Dedication

Dedicated to Sadie, Charles H. and
Benjamin Lewis: heroes.

[signature]

SADIE'S BOYS

LARRY LEWIS

SHIRES ❦ PRESS

Manchester Center, Vermont

SADIE'S BOYS

Copyright © 2017 by Larry Lewis

ISBN: 978-1-60571-388-5

First Edition: October 2017

SHIRES ✿ PRESS

4869 Main Street
P.O. Box 2200
Manchester Center, VT 05255
www.northshire.com

Building Community, One Book at a Time
A family-owned, independent bookstore in Manchester Ctr., VT, since 1976 and Saratoga Springs, NY since 2013. We are committed to excellence in bookselling. The Northshire Bookstore's mission is to serve as a resource for information, ideas, and entertainment while honoring the needs of customers, staff, and community.

CONTENTS

Preface

SOMETIME IN 1970, WHILE A JUNIOR IN HIGH SCHOOL, I was sitting in my room in my family's apartment in Queens. My father, Benjamin Lewis, came home from work, came into my room and tossed me a book.

"Here, read this."

I saw that the book was about an incident in World War II.

"I was there."

Like most kids my age growing up in the '60s, we would talk about, "What did your father do in the war?" My generation would learn either a little or a lot about our fathers' experiences in the war. It seemed that one's dad's propensity to talk was inversely proportional to how much combat he'd experienced. If, like some in my family, time in the "service" was about being on a tropical island, far from the fighting, then you spoke about those war years for the rest of your life. One of my relatives began almost every conversation with, "When I was in the service." However, if like my dad you fought your way across Europe and ended up in a German POW camp, you rarely if ever opened up.

When I'd ask my dad over the years about his time in the war I'd usually get one-word answers – or no response, which was odd because we were otherwise very close. My cherished memories include long conversations about almost any topic. But I never heard him start a conversation about the war and never, ever, did he utter a word about his brother. So when my dad tossed me a book that described a failed raid by American troops on a POW camp he was at in 1945 Germany, I got a rare glimpse into one slice of his time "in the service."

Another memory. I was very young, and my family, grandparents, and uncle, aunt, and cousins all lived in Brooklyn. My grandparents, Hyman and Sadie Lewis, lived at 1537 East 4th Street. By the time war broke out they had moved to 2365 65th Street, the home I remember: the brick stoop that led up to a solid wooden door. Aunt Perle, my father's sister, and her husband Seymour lived near them.

My grandparents' house was old, dusty, and filled with ancient furniture and framed photographs. I vividly remember one photo in particular, as do my brother and cousin, both named Charlie in honor of my father's brother Charles Haskel, who was killed in the war.

The photograph was taken in December 1943 at Mitchel Field,

Long Island. Grandpa Hyman, wearing a suit and standing proudly at attention in front of a US Army officer, is receiving my uncle Charlie's Silver Star for bravery in action. I think one reason the image has stuck with me is because grandpa Hyman didn't wear suits. He was usually in his easy chair, casually dressed, smoking a cigar, maybe drinking a glass of booze. He was smart and so funny that when I visited, I would laugh from the moment I saw him until I left. While I don't have the medal award photo, my brother's and cousin's memories of it, the account in the *Brooklyn Eagle,* and the fact that I have Lieutenant Charles Lewis' Silver Star in my home confirm my recollection of the event.

This story is an account of war heroes, but it is also the tale of my grandma Sadie. I only learned last year, while doing ancestry research, that Sadie's given name was actually Sarah. Sadly, women like Sadie were left out of most reports about World War II, or mentioned only in a supportive role. The work of women in the factories, Rosie the Riveters, has been told. An excellent book recounts the experiences of women who worked on the Manhattan Project[1]. But a woman taking on the establishment was so rare that you never heard much about that. All I can say is that I would not have wanted to be a politician confronted by my grandmother in her quest to find her two missing-in-action (MIA) sons.

In the 1990s, as relatives, including my grandparents, passed away, I ended up with a treasure trove of letters and documents that Sadie had kept. As an exercise to read everything and to preserve their contents, I transcribed all of the documents. And I realized that I had a true American story. I'm writing this during an election season. Often politicians will say things like, "I will fight for you." They do not use the word "fight" properly.

- Flying 100 feet off the surface of the ocean at 200 miles per hour while enemy planes above and naval ships and shore batteries below are shooting at you–*that's fighting.*
- Running at full speed at an enemy with your rifle with fixed bayonet while that enemy is trying to do the same to you–*that's fighting.*
- Refusing to just accept that your sons are missing and writing to government and the army officials until you get an answer-*that's fighting.*

How to honor the sacrifices of my father, uncle, and grandmother? The answer is to keep their memory alive and tell their story. This book uses actual letters and documents supplemented with historical background to fill in the narrative. May the world never forget their sacrifices to keep us free.

Sadie and Charlie circa 1925.

Chapter 1

Hyman and Sadie Lewis, 1941

MY GRANDPARENTS WERE POOR. Of course most people at the end of the Great Depression were poor. I always wondered how they made ends meet. My grandmother and her sons worried about money all the time.

Hyman's family came to the US in 1886 from London, England. Their origins before England are lost to history. I do know that Hyman was born in London, England and that census documents indicate that his parents were born in "Russia Poland." Hyman was the oldest of nine brothers. In later years when the whole family got together it was a rollicking time, with laughter,

The nine Lewis brothers.
Grandpa Hyman is in the first row, far left.

drinking, and lots of warmth. Hyman attended college for a year, which was most unusual for a poor immigrant. Sometime in the early 1900s, while living over a store in the Lower East Side, Hyman walked into a recruiting office and joined the Cavalry. Apparently it took some time for Hyman to be missed, and then some time for his family to find out where he was. It turns out that because Hyman was literate, he was made a clerk. He was posted in Virginia and indeed did ride horses. After a year or so, his parents bought him out of the army, as was the custom.

Sadie was born Sarah Roderfer (actually Ruderfer) in New York City in 1881, her parents having come to the US also from Russia, at the crest of the great wave of Eastern European Jewish immigration. Sadie's grandfather was Charles Talmud, for whom my uncle Charles was named. Charles Talmud's wife was "Perl," for whom my aunt Perle, Charles's and Ben's sister, was named. Everyone in the family used the Perle spelling for my aunt, but her given name was Riva Pearl Lewis.

Family lore has it that Hyman and Sadie were engaged for seven years, waiting until Hyman could support his wife. They were married November 24, 1918. Charles was born October 19, 1919 followed by Perle on May 25, 1922 and my father Benjamin, March 12, 1925.

Hyman made his living in the wholesale egg business. But just as the country was emerging from the Great Depression, his business was failing. He had to look for work, which Charles would mention in his frequent letters home in 1942. Charles graduated from James Madison High School in Brooklyn in 1936. From then until 1939, he attended City College part time and worked part time. In 1939 he switched to Brooklyn College, and by 1941, with Charles still in school, Perle was working and Ben was at Lincoln High School and had a job as a clerk. The kids were all contributing to the family's income when war broke out.

Hyman Lewis' discharge papers from the US Cavalry,
April 26, 1905.

Chapter 2

The Country Goes to War

MY BROTHER CHARLES DIDN'T INHERIT THE MATH GENE, but he has a gift with words. He captured what happened on December 7, 1941 as a columnist for the *Ottawa Citizen*[2], writing in 1991, on Remembrance Day (our Veteran's Day):

> "*On December 7, 1941 my father Benjamin Lewis was 15 [sic] years old. That Sunday morning he was sitting in the front room of my grandparent's home in Brooklyn, listening to the radio and acting as a lookout. In the back room, his older brother Charlie was running a poker game. The lookout probably wasn't necessary. My grandfather was one of the few people I knew who*

actually approved of gambling. But I suspect the idea of having a younger brother 'watching the street' just added to the artificial mood of danger. It was very much a Brooklyn scene – a bunch of the boys acting out the tough-guy image while the kid out front kept an eye on things. Years later, a family friend who was sitting at that poker table remembered my father bursting into the game yelling, 'Hey! Where the hell is Pearl Harbor?'"

It's a common misconception that World War II hit the US unprepared and by surprise. Nothing could be further from the truth. My grandparents were avid newspaper readers and we grandchildren were always expected to be up on the news. So it is likely that news reported in *The New York Times* and the *Brooklyn Eagle* was well known to Sadie and Hyman.

The big local news in Brooklyn in November 1941 was the mayoral election between incumbent reformer Republican Fiorello La Guardia, who was the 99th mayor of the city, and machine Democrat William O'Dwyer. La Guardia was an FDR supporter and had the President's backing. My grandparents were life-long Democrats, but I find it hard to believe they would NOT have voted for La Guardia. But bigger news loomed over the election.

By November 1941, Nazi Germany had conquered virtually all of Europe and the German army was only a few miles from Moscow. Germans were also taking Yugoslavia and threatening the Middle East from the north and also from the East from North Africa. The British and Germans were locked in tight battles in Libya and Egypt. German U-boats prowled the Atlantic and merchant ships were being lost regularly, with loss of life. On November 4, a German torpedo sunk the US destroyer Reuben James, which itself had sunk at least one enemy U-boat [3]. The US Navy was at war in the Atlantic and sailors were being killed. The American lend-lease policy was sending equipment to both the UK and to the Soviets. Our factories had been running full tilt for a year or more to produce war materiel. In fact, the economy had mostly recovered from the Great Depression by the end of 1941, thanks to the war production.

Trouble was brewing in Asia too, however *New York Times* readers saw daily war communiques from Europe and North Africa, but not from Asia until the Japanese attacks. The Japanese had been in active combat in China since the mid-1930s. Relations between the US and Japan were at an all-time low, and most newspaper articles discussed when, and not if, we would go to war with Japan. American flyers and ground crews joined the fight against Japan in China as the famous "Flying Tigers." When a high-level Japanese envoy went to the US to speak to President Franklin Roosevelt and Secretary of State Cordell Hull, the newspapers reported it as a last ditch effort at diplomacy[4]. All over Asia, from Singapore to the Philippines, plans were coalescing among the Allied powers and culminating for war against Japan. But not everyone was so sure the conflict would come. Sir Keith Murdoch, an Australian newspaper publisher and father of Rupert Murdoch, said that Japan wouldn't press its expansion in the face of a united front of democracies[5]. How wrong he was!

The war effort in the US was great and growing. A leaked government report on December 5 predicted a 5-million-man army would be necessary by 1943, at a cost of $150 billion[6]. The draft had been reinstated in October of 1940. In November 1941, 250 aviation cadets had graduated amid calls for several hundred thousand more. Sadie likely read daily of training accidents involving crashes of military planes and the deaths of airmen. On a lighter note, a cartoon in the *Brooklyn Eagle* from November 7 of that year depicted two women watching airmen descending from the sky in parachutes. "I don't suppose those paratroops care that we can't get silk stockings anymore," one muses[7]. Shipment of the silk of the now-precious stockings had ceased with blockade of imports from Japan.

Darker news was beginning to intrude, hints of the atrocities by the Japanese and Germans that would be common knowledge by war's end. Many have said that, especially in reference to the systematic horrors of the Holocaust, that, "we didn't know." But clues of the mass-murder were there in 1941.

On November 6, a report circulated of Germans executing 300,000 Serbs[8]. Eight days later, German Propaganda Minister Joseph Goebbels said in a speech that all Jews were the enemy of Germany and that it was the government's business to finally finish with the Jews[9]. Around Thanksgiving, Dr. Joshua Lieberman, the rabbi of Temple Israel in Boston, said prophetically that the Jewish people would have "a tremendous reparations bill to present to the nations at the peace table. The Jewish people were the first victims[10]." He also described the deportations of millions to German concentration camps. Later, a headline announced the slaughter of "Rumania Jews" by Romanian troops – Romania was a German ally[11].

We knew.

Chapter 3

Charlie Joins the Fight: Basic Training

MY UNCLE CHARLES RECEIVED A TELEGRAM on January 1, 1942, ordering him to report for his army physical on Governor's Island on Saturday morning, January 3. But on January 2, a letter arrived from the Headquarters of the Southern New York Recruiting District Aviation Cadet Examining Board, 39 Whitehall Street, New York, NY:

> *"Referring to your recent application for appointment as an Aviation Cadet, this is your notification that you should present yourself at this office on Tuesday morning, January 6, 1942 at 8:00 A.M. for your board interview."*

The Whitehall Street draft board building is the same one Arlo Guthrie sings about in "Alice's Restaurant."

By a month after the attack on Pearl Harbor, the Japanese had also struck Guam and Truk islands and begun invasion of the Philippines. The day after Charlie visited Governor's Island, the Japanese army began a massive invasion in and around New Guinea to shore up the southern border of their new empire. Furthermore, by establishing bases in New Guinea, the Japanese could regularly disrupt sea and air traffic from the US to Australia. The battles to defeat the Japanese in New Guinea would be the most brutal fighting of World War II. Charlie would learn about the battle for New Guinea firsthand.

If people thought the US was unprepared for war with Japan, however Australia was essentially defenseless. Three crack Australian divisions were fighting the Germans in North Africa. Japan invaded Rabaul, on the island of New Britain, off the east coast of New Guinea, against a light defense from the outnumbered Australian troops. In fact, just a single fighter squadron defended the entirety of Australia. On January 20, 1942, seven ancient and overmatched Australian planes faced more than 100 Japanese fighter planes ("Zeros"). On the 24th Japanese troop ships landed at Rabaul, quickly defeating the Australians and executing five Australian officers. A few Australians survived briefly in the jungle but were soon captured. The Japanese also executed 180 Australian infantry. These events set the stage for Charlie's future combat assignment[12].

The United States Army Air Corps was not ready for the war that was just declared. Most of the material manufactured in the

US by 1941 was shipped to Britain and the Soviet Union. A few fighter planes made their way to China to support the Flying Tigers. The US had 800 competitive aircraft in 1941, while the British Royal Air Force (RAF) had nearly 2000 and the German Luftwaffe almost 4000. Significant numbers of the only advanced bomber in the US fleet, the B-17E, were not delivered until November 1941. At that time, most US aviators were second lieutenants and their only experience was from flight school. They would face Japanese and German air forces with significantly more flying and combat time. Germany attacked Poland in September 1939, but their pilots had seen combat since the Spanish Civil War in the mid-1930s. And the Japanese had invaded Manchuria in mid-1937 and were fighting in China when Pearl Harbor was attacked. A few American flyers with combat experience volunteered in the RAF and with General Chenault's Flying Tigers in China.

Apparently Charlie passed his physical and interview because by January 12 he headed south by train, traveling through Philadelphia. On that day the great boxer Joe Louis enlisted in the Army. How different a world it would be when heavy weight champion Muhammad Ali refused induction into the Army in the 1960s.

Two days later Charlie arrived in Dothan, Alabama. His ultimate destination was Maxwell Field in Montgomery, Alabama, about 100 miles northwest of Dothan. Probably due to overcrowding, the Army sent Charlie and other cadets to Dothan to begin their training. Charlie would be at Maxwell within a month. Maxwell traced its roots to 1910 when the Wright Brothers opened a flying school in Montgomery. In 1922 the airfield was renamed

Maxwell Field in honor of William Maxwell, an army pilot killed in a crash in the Philippines. The US government maintained some sort of training facility in the area, which waxed and waned as a function of funding. By the early 1930s a training program at Maxwell focused on pursuit (fighter) planes. By 1940, Maxwell Field became the Southeast Air Corps Training Center[13].

The US Army Air Force (USAAF) was established in June 1941. By November, it had 300,000 men, 22,524 of them officers[14]. Because of the rapid increase in size of the USAAF in 1941, instructors were scarce. They were quickly pulled from the civilian teaching ranks at high schools and colleges, but frequently the instructors lacked the technical knowledge of their subject matter. Charlie weighed in on instructor quality in a letter to Sadie in April when he was in navigator school.

"Anyway I am sick and tired of Maxwell Field. I am not learning anything here. The courses we take are dull, slowed down so the most backward Cadet can keep well up with it. It is very rare that I learn something new and worthwhile. For instance I take 5 classes a day and 3 on Saturdays. That means a test per class (we get a test at the end of each class). Counting my time in the pilot area I must have had (together with what I still have) 45 books to study from- I have never "cracked" a book as the saying goes. (That is never read an assignment.) Yet the lowest test mark I have is 85 - with more than half my marks in the 100s. I made 4 hundreds in math (4 total or final marks for 20 hrs broken into 5 parts each) (and) I made 4 hundreds in physics (same as math). These were

the two most interesting and difficult courses I had. Now all I take are idiotic courses taught by instructors who read the assignment the night before and have to ask the class what the course is all about because it is not their field. I should be proud of my marks but I'm not. Any imbecile could have hit the same grades."

This early letter is remarkable in a few ways. In 1936, Charlie essentially flunked out of City College after three semesters, doing particularly poorly in math and physics. Then in 1939, he went to Brooklyn College, where he avoided hard science and math. Yet, here in navigator school he aced every test and wrote that he was mostly bored. Fast forward to his time in combat. Charlie will have to navigate a B-17E at night, over 11,000-foot plus mountains and then over open sea, getting to an exact point at a specific time. The navigation will require real-time calculation of distance, speed, altitude, and compass direction. Any mistake over the course of 10 to 15 hours will be fatal to him and his crew. *Bad in math?*

Charlie's goal was to become a pilot, but he knew that was a long shot. Pilots had to have uncorrected 20/20 vision, and his right eye was deficient. In the event that an air cadet failed to make it as a pilot, navigator or bombardier assignments were alternatives. Charlie proceeded with training, fully knowing that navigator school was a fallback option.

Cadet flight training was reduced in 1940 to seven months and only 200 flight hours to meet a potential demand for military pilots. From June 30, 1940 to June 30, 1941, the Army Air Corps tripled from 51,165 to 152,125 men [15]. The large expansion explains why Charlie ended up in Dothan to start his training. All of the cadets had the opportunity to request specific assignments, like pilot or bombardier, but they all went through four weeks of basic training.

Charlie's basic training was in January, which explains the dearth of letters from him from that time. The training was mostly physical (127 hours out of 192) and included the usual marching, platoon drill, and company drill, but with no weapons or infantry training. Basic training covered personal hygiene, articles of war, military courtesy and some psychological and math testing. Charlie described a typical day:

"Our day is quite crowded. Up at 5:30 to meet Reveille at 5:50. Out again after making beds and shaving, washing, etc. at 6:20 for breakfast. Back again at 7:15. We clean the room at 7 and at 7:45 we go to drill until 8:45. At 9:00 we go to athletics until lunch. After lunch- which is at 11:20- we have a few minutes to clean our rooms and at 12:45 we go to class. Back from classes at 4:15 or 4:30 clean up, shine our shoes which are dirty again (the most comfortable I've ever had-2 pair) wash etc. for supper which is at 5:20. Back again around 6:20 we have an hour to read the bulletin board and visit. From 7:30 to 9:30 we are not permitted to leave our rooms. Theoretically there is time to read and write, however with cleaning your rifle, your shoes, the room, studying your lessons, writing out drill exercises, being called to special meetings and formations, etc. there is precious little time left. At 9:30 you are permitted to make your bed, shower, etc. (The bed during the day is

*made for airing) At 10:00 lights out or taps is blown. And
so to bed! ...On Sunday we usually have the morning off.
And a parade in the afternoon. Incidentally on alternate
days we have classes in the morning and the rest of the
schedule in the afternoon. As you can see we are quite
busy and the routine is a little tiresome by now."*

It strikes me as a child of the 1960s and a witness to the civil
rights movement that at no time did Charles Lewis, a Jewish kid
from Brooklyn, ever comment about Jim Crow or the obvious
segregation of Alabama in 1942. Jackie Robinson, stationed in
Texas, met Jim Crow laws head on, refusing to move to the back
of a bus, the area meant for blacks. It may be that Charlie spent
little or no time off the base and so did not experience the true rural
south. However, Charlie was also a child of poverty and the Great
Depression and money issues were pervasive in his (and later in
his brother's) letters home.

According to the 1940 census, the median annual income in the
US was $1368. Charlie, as an Aviation Cadet, earned $75 a month
with a uniform allowance of $150 a month. Indeed, one of
Charlie's first letters home, no doubt from his first time away from
home, discusses finances, noting the $6 deducted from his pay for
an athletics uniform. Charlie, along with Perle and Ben, were
expected to contribute to the family income. His siblings had jobs
when Charlie joined the AAF. Hyman wasn't working, so money
was really tight.

By February 1, Charlie was still in Dothan. Charlie noted that
the Army expected thousands of cadets to be passing through his

training area. He loved all the food and teased the family back home about the rationing that had just started. He wrote the mundane minutiae of life in an army barracks, listing his needs:

- ✓ Needles and strong thread (I broke the needle I had sewing a button on my overcoat-army short coat rather).
- ✓ Stationery I can buy here but stamps and post cards are very low.
- ✓ A nail file for these damn nails which have to be cleaned now.
- ✓ A bootblack to shine my shoes for me-I have to shine them 4 times a day.
- ✓ And of course money: One dollar please-for newspapers and Coca Cola which can only be bought for cash. Everything else you get on credit (and I am running out of money by now).
- ✓ All I need until pay day tho (I think) is one buck. If you can't spare it, skip it-I'll borrow somebody else's paper.

Meanwhile in Rabaul, the Japanese were building a virtually impregnable fortress[12]. The Japanese installed more than 400 ground-based anti-aircraft batteries as well as radar all over the island of New Britain to detect incoming Allied planes.

Fortunately I was raised with the Lewis clan and I know how to translate their sense of humor. Charlie wrote of his brother, "Congratulate Ben on his lousy marks. Glad I wasn't there to see them throw him out of school." He's being sarcastic – my father was an outstanding student. I was on the receiving end of comments like Charlie's when I was going to school.

A really good example of the Lewis sense of humor is a crazy letter Charlie sent to his sister complaining that she doesn't write often enough:

> *"Dear Poil, Very pleased ta get yer letta. Howz it you no write soona? Huh? I can no unnerstand how anyone iz a having a brother like da one youze got & iz no writing more."*

Pretty good mockery of what must have been a bit of his own Brooklyn accent. In fact an article in the *Brooklyn Eagle* stated that some incoming students to Brooklyn College would need to learn proper English (and presumably unlearn their Brooklynese!).

By February 1942, life was great for Charlie. Back home rationing had begun in earnest, but he was out of Brooklyn and well fed. While Charlie had struggled in college, now he was a great student, so classes were easy. He had time to write home. But he had two worries. One, his pilot physical was in two weeks and he had little hope that his right eye would pass muster. His second worry was always about money. One letter mentioned the six cents postage due on a package he received. He asked often about whether his dad had found work, but curiously, I have no record of him ever writing to his father. I have letters to Perle, Ben, and of course his mother. It may be that when Hyman's business failed in 1940-41, he had a nervous breakdown and was very fragile. In March Charlie wrote, *"I hope Dad gets something quickly as I know how things are and I feel very bad about them."* And then ominously a few days later, replying to a post-card he received from his mother, *"When you write about Dad please put it in a letter not a postcard. You can never tell."* Even a month later, Hyman had gone for a job interview in Elmira but was not successful. Meanwhile in the war in the Pacific, the first B-17 arrived in Australia on February 19[16].

At the end of basic training, the air cadets took several multi-day tests. These included a psychological evaluation, medical exams such as the dreaded vision test, and aptitude testing, which evaluated perceptual speed and accuracy, the ability to read and understand graphs and charts, motor coordination and dexterity, and steadiness under pressure [17].

"Graduation" was March 15 and Charlie would soon learn his fate. On March 22, his class moved on to "primary school" for pilots. He was left behind. He applied for a waiver (for his poor vision) but was denied. Ironically he wrote,

> *"I just wait around at Maxwell Field until the Board meets, hears my case ... and makes up its mind–assigns me–probably–to navigation and then I wait–probably again–another month here, before they send me to navigation school. I do not particularly care for this since I have never been particularly interested in finding my way around by use of maps, charts, etc. You know how I liked geography."*

Charlie started navigation school April 13.

By the end of April, Charlie was still at Maxwell Field, but a new problem developed. Apparently Sadie tried to get Charlie out of the army because of his chronically bad back. He mentions it in the negative in some of his letters, as in, "no problem with my back."

Charlie's response makes the issue pretty clear:

> *"This letter is written (instead of a postcard) because I remembered something you wrote that I neglected to comment upon. About that letter from the doctor. Don't ever send anything like that. If I even suspected why it was sent I would not come home. Don't you think that there are thousands of boys down here whose parents want them home as much as you do? We just can't do things like that. It isn't fair."*

Sadie was of course just acting out what many mothers were thinking at the time. If only they knew what was coming—Sadie apparently used the guilt trip on Charlie; she was a Jewish mother after all. She was upset with Charlie being upset with her! Charlie stood up to her:

> *"I received your letter today-the one about my hard letter. I don't blame you for feeling the way you do–if we were in each other's positions I might feel the same. All the same I think you'll agree that it was the first letter of its kind in all the time I've been writing and that's almost a letter a day. Not a bad percentage when I can usually find so many things to argue about. Anyway I think you should allow me one "blow up" in 3-1/2 months.*

Besides-not wishing to complain–things haven't been so easy down here. I know I should be grateful because I am in the best physical health of my life–but there are other things."

While all this was going on, US and Australians were bombing Rabaul, while on the ground the Japanese were beating and killing their POWs. Also at this time the 64th bomb squadron, Charlie's future home, had a new commanding officer, Captain Eugene Halliwill. His unit had one plane[17].

Charlie gave a glimpse of the home front in referring to the job of a cousin, Leo:

"He is working as a materiel checker in New Brunswick, NJ. He works 7 days a week. He has to get up at 4:30 AM since he has a 2 hour trip to work (and 2 hours back, of course). He gets home at 8:30 PM. He tells me that he hasn't had a day off in 5 weeks. When he asked for one they said, 'your country is at war. You have to sacrifice.' And as Leo said, 'what answer is there to that?' Good part is that he makes $75 a week."

At this time, the Lewis family back home was totally broke. Hyman had no work and Charlie's pay kept getting delayed. Charlie was the breadwinner.

Chapter 4

Navigator Training

IN JULY 1941, TURNER FIELD opened in Albany, Georgia as a navigator training center. Charlie arrived on May 22, 1942. On May 6, the Philippines were lost. Sgt. Irving Strobing was the last telegraph operator on Corregidor, Philippines. His final message, "The jig is up. Everyone here is bawling like a baby. They are piling dead and wounded in our tunnel. Arms weak from pounding keys. Long hours, no rest, short rations, standby..." Sgt. Strobing was held as a POW in Osaka main camp for 3 years, 7 months and survived the war[18]. May 6-7 was the battle of Coral Sea, where Japanese struck two US aircraft carriers. American planes rarely hit their targets, although US planes from Lexington and Yorktown did sink a Japanese carrier, Shoho.

The training at Turner would include flying in mostly Beech AT-7 aircraft and 500 hours of ground instruction along with air training. The ground instruction included courses in compass, drift meter, altimeter, plotting, log book, and weather. Air training had a minimum of 20 flights (total 100 hours) where the trainees had to learn rendezvous and conduct search and patrol exercises in the day and night. The night flights required celestial navigation[15].

Charlie raved about the food at Turner Field – lots of fresh fruits and vegetables. Although he passed his physical when he arrived, at 175 pounds, he needed to worry about weight gain. He commented that Ben, perennially too skinny, would do well at a place like Turner. Charlie estimated navigator training to take 6 months (pretty accurate). He described a typical day at Turner:

> *"We begin classes at 8 AM sharp. Stop at 11:50 for lunch and back again at 12:50 to 3:50. We have athletics from 4-5. Supper from 5:30 to 6:30. And most of us are in here doing our homework and studying from 7 PM to 9:30."*

He had a nice change of attitude about being a navigator: *"Well it is 7 PM and off to my work table. Who ever thought I would be working with maps spread all over my desk - and liking it."*

While Charlie was training, Allied forces stopped a Japanese invasion force from taking Port Moresby with heavy jungle fighting[19].

One letter that Charlie wrote to Perle survived, from May 1942.

My cousin Charlie, Perle's son, found the letter. The elder Charlie had the Brooklyn smart-aleck way about him, but also a closeness underneath the bravado. After explaining to his sister that he didn't buy a birthday card, he wrote the following poem:

"Hello sis- how's tings
I hope dat on yer boithday
Life brings
Happiness so true
And you'll never be blue
Especially in May
Since it's yer boithday"

Charlie thought his poem was as good as any of the cards he could have bought for 15 cents, he wrote, and by the way this one was free! He teased her some more and then asked her to tell Ben that if he didn't write once a week, he'd bash his head in the next time they were together. How sweet!

Sadie knew there was an element of risk even at this stage of Charlie's training. Fatal accidents happened at all points and in every type of aircraft. In 1942, about 500 fatal accidents involved trainers of some sort. Sadie wrote to Charlie about the dangers[20]. His response:

"You asked why there are so many crashes. I can give you a rough idea. In the small ships (just a pilot) it is understandable. They fly at such great speeds 300-400 and over miles per hour that wrong handling doesn't give you time to correct yourself. Besides, they take off

and land at terrific speeds–from 120-185 mph. You can
see where a person would have to be in the <u>best</u> physical
condition to bring them in safely. But in the big ships, the
bombers, it is a different story. The ships are big enough
to ride smoothly and 7 times out of 10 when there is an
accident, it's the fault of the <u>navigator</u>. Because he didn't
figure the right altitude and they hit a mountaintop, or he
got lost and they ran out of gas–or some such reason. So,
my safety will depend 70% on how well <u>I learn now</u>."

On June 10, Charlie was fitted for an officer's uniform. He was still working very hard, with demanding courses, and he no longer complained about the work being too easy! He fully realized that this training meant life or death. Over the next few weeks, he mentioned a meteorology course, and later about learning celestial navigation. Cadets were flunking out, with a 25% failure rate on one test. He was hanging in so far.

Meanwhile, the Japanese invaded New Caledonia, Fiji, and Samoa. The battle of Midway began. On July 6, the Japanese invaded Guadalcanal.

Charlie mentioned on July 26 that graduation was in five or six weeks. He'd not had a day off or a furlough home since he left on the train in January. Although Charlie's class graduation was announced for September 2, 1942, postmarks indicate that he'd visited Louisville, Kansas City, and Fort Leavenworth, Kansas in late August. I presume he flew to these places on training missions. He noted all the "help-wanted" signs he saw in his travels.

August 28 was a turning point. "Now it can be told-as the song goes. Last night I flew my last mission as a cadet. I have a total of about 100 flying hours. About 30 of them at night," Charlie wrote. At this time General McArthur named Major General George Kenney as commander of the (all US) 5th Air Force[21].

Unknown to the cadets or anyone back home, the Japanese on New Britain had decided to get rid of all of their prisoners. They loaded 845 POWs and 208 civilians onto the Montevideo Maru, heading for imprisonment on Hainan Island. Shortly after leaving port, the USS Sturgeon submarine torpedoed the Montevideo, sinking it in 11 minutes[22]. Most of the prisoners were lost. The Australian rock group Midnight Oil mentions the singer's grandfather "going down on the Montevideo" in the song "In the Valley." The lyrics incorrectly claim that a "rising sun" (Japanese) sent him to his rest. It was the stars and stripes.

Graduation from Turner did not grant Charlie a much-desired furlough, because his next letter was from Tallahassee, Florida. The good news was that as an officer he was getting paid $225/month. The bad news was that a visit home was still months away.

After several days of travel, Charlie arrived in Fort Myers, Florida, home of Eglin Field and its bombing and gunnery ranges, to finish training. "Today we had code class, a lecture, athletics. Then we went skeet shooting, played ping pong, went for a swim...," he wrote of his first full day. From Eglin, Charlie took part in cross-country flights, warning his family that he might show up unexpectedly at their door at any time. It was September and for a Jewish boy from Brooklyn, Charlie must have missed the

High Holy Days with his family.

The only hint of Charlie's Jewish background came in one letter:

> *"...there was no allowance made here for the (Jewish) holidays. There is no synagogue in this town-the nearest one is about 100 miles away. So about 10 or 15 boys had a service of their own, in the chapel on the field. They weren't given passes to go to the nearest synagogue though they requested same."*

Good old open-minded US Army!

In order to fly, Charlie had to move to Hotel Royal Palm in Fort Meyers to be near a small base where the planes were housed. He would be flying B-26, twin-engine bombers. The B-26 had a poor safety record, but Charlie never mentioned it. During this time Charlie finished bombardier training. Every member of the crew also was trained in gunnery, which would turn out to be extremely important, as he unwittingly foreshadowed events: *"Oh yes. Operating a power turret (machine gun) I set the range <u>record</u> for <u>consecutive hits </u>on a moving target the other day. Not my job but handy to know. I've always made good bombing scores-so far."* By October 9, his crew had been assembled. They were rated #1 at their base.

Finally, Charlie received a leave to visit his family that would start on November 4. He couldn't afford to fly, so he took the train from Fort Myers. What would turn out to be a "last picture" of

Charlie in uniform shows him at home on the same stoop where he was photographed as a young boy.

Charlie's leave was seven days, including travel time. When Charlie returned from leave, he split his time between Eglin Field and Fort Myers. His last letter from Florida was dated December 8. Soon after, he was on a train heading west, destination San Francisco.

His letters home reveal the route: Montgomery, Alabama; El Paso, Texas; Phoenix, Arizona; and Los Angeles on December 19. Arrived San Francisco December 20, at Hamilton Field. This was where Charlie and his crew met their B-17E for their further flight west. They arrived in Honolulu on December 30, and arrived in Australia January 4, 1943.

While details of Charlie's trip across the Pacific Ocean are missing, the trip across the sea of the B-17, "Taxpayer's Pride," was described in the flight diary of flight engineer Frank Hohmann [23]. Taxpayer's Pride got off to a bad start. During maintenance in California, the crew witnessed a female mechanic accidently walk into a rotating propeller, she was killed instantly.

Taxpayer's Pride left Hamilton Field on August 8, 1943 but returned to California because of a sick crewmember. Three days later they departed, landing on Canton Island on August 13. The next day, the plane left for Nadi, in the Fiji Islands. Halfway out, the crew decided to turn back to Canton Island due to a propeller that would not respond to pitch control; this was the same propeller that had killed the mechanic back in California. A few days later, a wrong replacement part arrived from Hawaii. Some local English engineers jury-rigged a fix to use the "wrong part." The crew test-flew the plane with the new part and then finally arrived at Mareeba, Australia on August 25.

There is another record of the journey of a B-17 and its crew from California to Australia[24]. That plane reached Hickam Field, Hawaii in 15 hours, then flew on to Christmas Island. The navigator could not see land and had only a sextant, seeing stars (when visible), and a compass. Next stop: Canton Island, then Fiji. One more landing in New Caledonia and finally to Brisbane, Australia. Total flying time: 46 hours.

The plane that Charlie flew, the B-17E, was much improved from the original model A, with a better electrical system and additional armor plating. The plane added larger rudders and flaps and a streamlined nose. Changing from the original Wright 1820-51 to Wright 1820-65 engines added power. The model E also had self-sealing fuel tanks, a tail gunner, and rectangular side windows for better waist gunner visibility. The new model was equipped with Bendix remote-control belly turret guns. Finally, the bombardier was positioned below and forward in the plane, with the navigator seated directly behind him. Either navigator or bombardier could operate the nose gun [16,25]. The proximity of the bombardier and navigator to each other explains why their bodies would later be found together on a beach on New Britain.

Last photograph of 2nd Lieutenant Charles H. Lewis at home in Brooklyn before shipping out to the Pacific, November-December, 1942.

B-17[25]

Chapter 5

Charlie's Introduction to Combat

The 64th Bomb Squadron

CHARLIE AND HIS CREW WERE MEMBERS of the 43rd Bomb Group, 64th Bomb Squadron; a bomb group composed of several smaller squadrons. The unit immediately relocated to Port Moresby, New Guinea where they would stay for the rest of Charlie's time. Bruce Gamble's book[12] described Port Moresby as "rain every day, hordes of mosquitoes. Airmen fatigued, lack of sleep. No permanent buildings, bad food and no fighter plane support." A day after Charlie arrived in Australia, the 64th Bomb Squadron commander Major Allen Lindbergh (no relation to the famous aviator Charles Lindbergh)[26] was killed in action, a rude welcome. But because Charlie arrived in Australia on January 4 and his commander's last mission flew from Port Moresby on January 5, they probably never met.

Lindbergh flew from 7-Mile Drome near Port Moresby on January 5 with a crew of nine and two observers, Major Jack Bleasdale and Brigadier General Kenneth Walker. Although General Kenney had ordered an attack on Rabaul for the 5th, Walker disagreed with his boss about the timing of the mission. Kenney wanted it at dawn, which meant flying in the dark to the target. Walker worried about the large number of crashes that had recently occurred during night flights. So he disobeyed orders and led (as observer on Lindbergh's plane) a mission with six B-17s and six Liberators, arriving over their targets at noon. The low-altitude attack also put them in easy range of Rabaul's coastal guns and Japanese fighter planes[12,16].

The flight from Port Moresby left at 0848 and arrived at the target in Simpson Bay at 1200. The Liberators arrived first, dropping their bombs but encountering a large number of enemy fighters, several of which chased Lindbergh's plane, leaving the left engine smoking. The plane was never seen again. Of the eleven on board, only co-pilot Captain Benton Daniel and Major Bleasdale were listed as POWs; the others were listed as killed in action. Bleasdale and Daniel successfully bailed out of their plane, but Daniel was captured in January. Interrogation records from February and March indicate that both men were POWs, and their names also appear on a document from July 1943. Bleasdale did not survive captivity but his cause of death was never determined. A Japanese report from March 1943 indicates that Daniel was interrogated about the technical details of a B-17. A Catholic priest held near Rabaul reported that Daniel was sent to Kavieng, which if true meant that he was most likely executed, as were all the prisoners in that section. The executions were subject to war crimes investigations.

During the same raid with General Walker, Captain (later Major) Jean A. Jack flew a plane that sustained damage and was forced into a water landing near Urasi Island off the coast of New Guinea. When the crew of Captain Jack's plane used a life raft to reach land on the island, they met friendly natives.

Meanwhile, search planes saw Captain Jack's bomber and signaled a Qantas Airlines flying boat to pick up what the searchers thought would be General Walker and his crew. In fact, a film crew accompanied the flying boat to capture the rescue of the famous general.

"Where's the general?" asked a member of the crew of the flying boat as the hatch opened.

"What general?" Captain Jack replied.

"General Walker."

"I don't know, but there's no General Walker here!"

Had Walker survived, he would have likely received a reprimand for disobeying orders. Instead, Walker was awarded the Congressional Medal of Honor posthumously[16].

In Charlie's January 4 letter, the only one from Australia, he of course didn't know what was about to happen to Major Lindbergh.

It was the first and only mention of Ben's thinking of joining the navy. That didn't happen, and Ben would have a very different fate than his brother.

Charlie's 64th Squadron officially transferred to Port Moresby January 20. He was still in Australia on the 9th, but may have moved to New Guinea by the 14th and was definitely there on the 28th. That day New York City was digging out from a snowstorm and coping with stymied trash removal. Also back home, the *Brooklyn Eagle* had a story about Lieutenant George F. Callahan from South Ozone Park, Queens. General Kenney awarded Lt. Callahan a Silver Star. Lt. Callahan had completed 50 missions by January 1943 and he'd shipped over to Australia shortly after the attack on Pearl Harbor[27].

In New Guinea, things were difficult in a different way. For example, the 43rd Bomb Group had nominally 50 B-17s but usually 20 were being overhauled, 15 or so were used for reconnaissance, and only about 13 were available to fly combat missions.

In September 1942, when General Kenney formed the 5th Air Force, he was concerned about the poor performance of high altitude bombing; bombers hit their targets only about one percent of the time. Raid after raid brought little or no damage, especially to Japanese ships. So Majors William G. Benn and Kenneth McCullar perfected a technique known as "skip bombing," which the RAF had used in the war in Europe. Similar to the idea of skipping a stone across a pond, the idea was to fly as low as 200 feet above the water and release the bombs in the direction of the target, so that impact was more likely than when dropped from many thousands of feet straight down. The 64th Bomb Group first used the strategy on October 20 and 22 on raids and hit two small ships. The attacking planes would rapidly descend to 200 feet and then launch their bombs with delayed fuses. Many trials were conducted off the coast of Port Moresby to perfect skip bombing[16].

James T. Murphy[24] helped develop the technique of skip bombing and then had a successful career as an engineer for NASA after the war. He compared the problems encountered with skip bombing to being as challenging as those of developing the Saturn V rocket, which sent astronauts to the moon. Variables that the 43rd Bomb Squadron had to consider in skip bombing included the length of delay of the bomb fuse, height to drop the bomb (so it would skip and not sink), speed of the aircraft, and angle of approach.

After Major Lindbergh was killed on January 5, 1943 the 64th Bomb Squadron was led by Captain Charles Giddings. Captain Giddings would earn a Silver Star for bravery and survived the war. He also survived a mid-air collision shortly after take-off on April of 1943. Giddings would command the Squadron again briefly in April.

Chapter 6

Charlie in New Guinea

CHARLIE COMPLAINED IN LETTERS home from this time that he hadn't received any mail from them since leaving Florida, even though he was duly sending money home. He mentioned a bit about his flight from Hawaii to Australia. They apparently landed at a number of islands for re-fueling, which he couldn't name. The trains he rode in were "poor in comparison to our own." By January 14 he wrote that he still hadn't received any mail. He was gaining weight, approaching 200 pounds! His last letter from Australia was dated January 20. He had no place to spend money, so he cabled $175 home (a pretty large sum for the Lewis family).

Change was coming to the 64th Bomb Squadron in Australia. Captain (later Major) Ken McCullar replaced Giddings on January 15. By month's end, the squadron moved to Port Moresby on the south side of New Guinea. The larger organization, the 43rd Bomb Group, which included the 63rd and 64th Bomb Squadrons, were busy. The mission of the 43rd was to neutralize the Japanese troop ships, fighters, bombers, and convoys of supply and combat ships on Rabaul. The Japanese effort was to establish a foothold on the northern part of New Guinea, having failed to dislodge the Allies from the southern part of the island. Finally, the Japanese used Rabaul to project their dominance in the southern Pacific, including denying access to the sea lanes for the Allies[16].

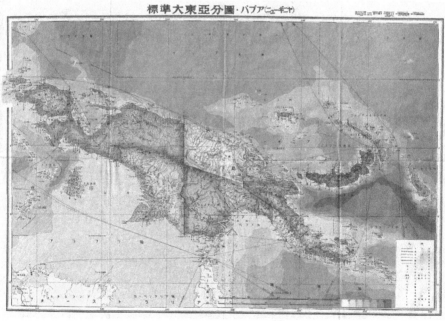

標準大東亞分圖・パプア(ニューギヤ)

Map of New Guinea[28].

At the end of January, Charlie went to the place that is today the independent nation of Papua New Guinea. In 1943, Australia administered the area of conflict. The Allies' base was in and around Port Moresby, today the capital of Papua New Guinea. The Japanese built a base in Lae, almost due north of Port Moresby. To attack Lae or Rabaul from Port Moresby, Allied planes had to fly due north over the Owen Stanley Mountain Range into the Bismarck Sea and then turn east. The mountain range was 11,000 to 13,000 feet high. A few passes through the mountains enabled the planes to fly a bit lower. One such pass was the Kokoda Trail that navigators like Charlie would attempt to follow on their way to Lae or to Rabaul, 500 miles from Port Moresby. This track was also the path that the Japanese attempted to use to attack Port Moresby by land. Charlie was not in the infantry or marines, but he certainly was aware of the terrible toll that ground combat had taken on soldiers fighting in the jungles of New Guinea[21].

Another battle Charlie would fight every time he flew to Rabaul was against the weather. The Solomon Sea separates New Guinea from New Britain. On a good day, the planes would encounter rain, updrafts, and clouds. The Solomon Sea, in an intertropical convergence zone, produces ultra-severe thunderstorms with cloud tops above 40,000 feet, well beyond the maximum altitude of a B-17[12].

The allies paid a high price to keep Port Moresby. On July 22, 1942, a large Japanese force landed at Gona Mission near Buna, determined to climb the Owen Stanley Mountains by land using the Kokoda Trail to attack and destroy Port Moresby, a straight distance of 120 miles. If this wasn't challenging enough, the

Japanese soldiers had to traverse some of the densest jungle in the world, ascending mountains 11,000 feet high. They got to within 30 miles of Port Moresby when American and Australian infantry stopped them. It was mid-September, two months after the Japanese had landed in Gona. By December 9, Allied fighters recaptured Gona and had Buna under siege by January 2. All resistance in the Papua Territory had fallen by January 23[21].

While Charlie finished his training in Australia[29] through most of January, the 43rd Bomb Group was busy[17]. Their activities for January 1943 contrast with news from back home.

FRIDAY, 1 JANUARY, 1943: B-24s and B-17s bombed the airfields at Rabaul, New Britain Island and Gasmata Island in the Bismarck Archipelago and Lae, New Guinea and attacked shipping at Rabaul. A reconnaissance mission revealed more than 80 ships in Rabaul, which agreed with intelligence garnered from "Ultra," the super-secret American group that broke the Japanese code.

Sadly many of the crews that went out on a mission would become Japanese POWs. Back home, *New York Times* readers received instructions on how to write letters to captives of the Japanese, and the families received detailed instructions from the Red Cross. Short, printed letters went from the American Red Cross to the International Red Cross in Geneva and then finally (hopefully) to the prisoner in a camp[30]. The family of one of Charlie's crewmate's family will need this information.

SATURDAY, 2 JANUARY, 1943: The 5th Air Force continued their efforts against the Japanese as A-20s, B-24s, B-25s, and B-26s hit the airfields and targets at Lae and Gasmata Island. A-20s were light two-engine bombers with crews of three. B-24s were heavy bombers and were also known as Liberators. B-25s were medium twin-engine bombers. B-26s were also twin-engine bombers also known as Marauders. On the ground, US and Australian forces finally overran Buna Mission on the North side of New Guinea. A Liberator with a full bomb load crashed into debris on the 7-Mile air strip at Port Moresby, killing seven crew members. Ground personnel were decorated for their efforts to save three of the Liberator's crew.

Families famous and not famous had to deal with sad news from the war. In Brooklyn, the nephew of New York State Supreme Court justice William R. Wilson learned that staff sergeant Raynor H. Wilson was killed in action "in Western Europe." Raynor's late father Frank Wilson was a former National League umpire[31].

SUNDAY, 3 JANUARY, 1943: In New Guinea missions continued when P-40s strafed troops in the waters off Buna and US and Australian ground forces finished their activities in the nearby Buna Missions area. B-26s, along with a single B-24, bombed Madang and an A-20 hit Salamaua. A lone B-24 strafed the airfield on Gasmata Island.

Not everyone back home was as fully engaged in what was happening overseas as Sadie. Mrs. Eddie (Adelaide) Rickenbacker said that "women of leisure" who ignore the fact that the nation is at war needed to be shocked into assuming wartime responsibilities[32]. Eddie Rickenbacker was America's most famous air ace from World War I. In October of 1942, his B-17 ran out of fuel and ditched in the Pacific. Rickenbacker and his crew survived 24 days in rafts eating birds and

drinking rain water until natives rescued them (one crew-member died). Rickenbacker's survival record stood until US Olympian Louis Zamperini and pilot Russell Philips survived 47 days in a raft in the Pacific. Laura Hillenbrand's "Unbroken" tells this amazing story of survival[33,34].

MONDAY, 4 JANUARY, 1943 Charlie's first letter from Australia. Preparations for an allied offensive got underway near the Sanananda Point area as B-26s pounded and A-20s and B-25s hit airfields, AA positions and buildings at Lae. B-24s, on single-plane flights, bombed the Lae airfield and attacked schooners off Gasmata Island and Cape Kwoi.

That public opinion was on the side of the troops is nicely expressed in this cartoon from the *Brooklyn Eagle*[35]. The cartoon shows a civilian "hoarder" as a snake. A hoarder was someone who did not contribute their personal goods to the war effort. Most people freely donated spare items for war materiel production.

THE SNAKE IN THE GRASS

TUESDAY, 5 JANUARY, 1943: Australian infantry and armored elements reached Soputa and US forces of the 128th Infantry Regiment started northwest along the coast toward Tarakena. There were preliminary moves towards an all-out assault on Sanananda. The Air Force did its part with assaults at the Sanananda Point area and A-20s and B-25s hit the airfield at Lae. Six B-17s and six B-24s bombed the harbor, shipping, and the airfield at Rabaul. Two B-17s were lost, one taking Brigadier General Kenneth Walker, Commanding General V Bomber Command to his death.

Charlie was destined to become a Brooklyn Jewish war hero. However the first was Meyer Levin. The family of Sergeant Meyer Levin, who was killed in action February 8, 1942 in the East Indies, learned that their son was posthumously awarded a Silver Star for bravery. Sergeant Levin was one of the first Americans to see action after war was declared. Brooklyn held a Meyer Levin Day, and he became the first Jewish American war hero. Charlie also posthumously received the Silver Star[36].

WEDNESDAY, 6 JANUARY, 1943: Support for the battles near the Sanananda Point area continued with B-26 bombing runs and A-20s attack on the Lae Airfield. In the Bismarck Archipelago, B-17s, B-24s, B-26s and P-38s attacked a convoy southwest off the coast of New Britain heading for Lae; a B-24 bombed the airfield on Gasmata Island. Charles Giddings was a future commander of the 64th Squadron and a pilot our Charlie would fly with. On this day, Giddings' B-17 failed to hit any ships in an enemy convoy and then was attacked by three Japanese fighters. Most of Giddings crew was injured and the plane lost an engine, yet Giddings managed to return to Port Moresby.

Sadie would learn later that one of her sons listed as missing in action was in fact alive. Likewise Mrs. Fredrick W. White received word that her son, Emile Fog, was not in fact missing in action as a telegram from the War Department had notified her. On October 12, 1942, Emile Fog's ship, the Destroyer Meredith, was sunk while delivering supplies to US troops fighting on Guadalcanal. Mrs. White had received a letter from her son 10 days prior to the dire government telegram, saying that he was alive and well. Emile and four crewmates floated on a mattress for two days until rescue[37].

THURSDAY, 7 JANUARY, 1943: A Japanese convoy bound for Lae from New Britain was again attacked by heavy, medium, and light bombers and fighters, along with Royal Australian Air Force (RAAF) planes, in the Solomon Sea off Finschhafen and during its progress off the south coast of the Huon Peninsula through Huon Gulf to Lae. Despite the heavy air attack by the Allies, the Japanese convoy reached its destination. Fighters also attacked Lae Airfield.

Just as Sadie would learn one of her sons was a POW, another Brooklyn mother, Mrs. Anna Shure, learned that her son Lieutenant Paul Shure was on a list of POWs in the Philippines. Lt. Shure was a 12-year army veteran. The Japanese also held Brooklynite Lieutenant John Paul Flynn, a 25-year army veteran. Shure was sent to Osaka Main Camp in Japan, where he survived three years, seven months, one of the longest captivities under the Japanese[38].

In Casablanca, Morocco, Allied leaders met and agreed that 85 perecent of Allied resources would be devoted to the war in Europe. The meeting in Casablanca reinforced agreements from just after Pearl Harbor called the "Europe First" strategy[39]. So for Charlie and all his fellow airmen, resources would always be limited as they took on the Japanese Empire.

FRIDAY, 8 JANUARY, 1943: About 100 American and RAAF aircraft continued pounding the Japanese convoy as it unloaded about 4,000 reinforcements at Lae. Japanese fighter cover and Allied aircraft continued fierce aerial combat. 2nd Lieutenant Jose L. Holgain was a navigator on a B-17 and in this attack he was operating one of the two nose turret 0.30 caliber machine guns on the right side of the plane. The gun Holgain was firing over-heated and seized up, so the navigator attempted to swap out the broken gun with the good gun on the left side. While struggling to move the working gun over, several errant rounds were shot into the roof of the plane, just missing the bombardier. Many apologies from Holgain followed after the mission was complete.

Sadie would receive and send letters to two sons overlapping with a time when they both were declared missing in action. In Brooklyn, Corporal Howard Russell's mother received a letter from her son saying that he was well and happy and waiting for the day that "this thing is over." Russell was stationed in New Guinea. Alas, the letter arrived after Mrs. Russel learned that her son had been killed in "a bomber[40]."

SATURDAY, 9 JANUARY, 1943: Charlie was riding the rails in Australia, avoiding the major cities. US bombers and fighters, along with RAAF aircraft, continued to attack the convoy as it left Lae. Airfields, supply dumps, and troop concentrations at Lae and at Salamaua were also hit. In four days of attacks on this convoy, two transports were sunk, several vessels damaged, and about 80 aircraft destroyed.

While the airmen fought in the skies, the folks back home learned about the difficult time seamen were having in the war. On this day was a report of the survival of an 18-year-old seaman first class (name not reported) from California. On November 14 and 15, 1942, the seaman's

ship had been hit and sunk off Guadalcanal. He and a shipmate, "Red," floated for two days and then washed ashore on Guadalcanal. The two managed to avoid Japanese patrols and lived off coconuts until December 5, when they spotted the American lines. However, the two men had to get past the Japanese. Red found a rifle and opened fire, killing some Japanese but getting killed himself. In the melee´, the seaman was able to crawl past the Japanese to the safety of American troops[41].

SUNDAY, 10 JANUARY, 1943: Allied aircraft operating over the Solomon Sea south of New Britain Island continued to attack vessels of the Japanese convoy that departed Lae. In New Guinea, supply dumps and AA positions in the Lae area were also bombed. The 13th Bombardment Squadron (Dive), 3rd Bombardment Group (Dive) with B-25s transferred from Charters Towers, Queensland, Australia to Port Moresby, New Guinea thus moving these air groups closer to the fighting.

US Public opinion was not favorable towards the Japanese even including Japanese US citizens. Sadie was not much different in this regard as some of her later letters suggest. In Washington, DC, a congressional committee received reports complaining that Japanese Americans in internment camps were getting "huge quantities" of surplus food, while surrounding communities were subjected to rationing. Representative Harry Sheppard (D, Cal) personally inspected the camps and found the rumors groundless. Furthermore, Sheppard reported that internees asked how "in a democracy citizens can be interned[42]."

MONDAY, 11 JANUARY, 1943: A short note from Charlie, still in Australia, reported good health and no action in New Guinea. During this brief lull in the fighting, several crews got a furlough to Australia.

Charlie, Ben, and their father Hyman would have had strong opinions about a story from New York as all three were known to enjoy an alcoholic beverage. Mayor La Guardia commended a bartender who refused to sell beer to an 18-year-old sailor. "If 18-year-olds are old enough to fight, they ought to be able to get a drink," said the sailor. The Lewises would have supported the sailor[43].

TUESDAY, 12 JANUARY, 1943: The air war in and around New Guinea resumed as B-24s bombed the Finschhafen and Madang areas. The US destroyer Monssen was sunk off the Solomon Islands.

Mrs. Mons Monssen of Brooklyn sponsored the ship, which was launched May 16, 1940. It was named for her late husband, Congressional Medal of Honor winner Lt. Monssen, for heroism on the battleship Missouri in 1904. Mrs. Monssen lived off her husband's pension and nearly lost her home to foreclosure. She was invited to the launching of the USS Monssen in 1940, but couldn't afford to attend the ceremony in California. Finally, The Navy League provided travel funds[44].

WEDNESDAY, 13 JANUARY, 1943: The Allied Air Force continued their support of the ground troops on New Guinea. A-20s bombed and strafed the Sanananda Point area and forces along the Sanananda track. Heavy and medium bombers hit dock facilities at Lae and airfields at Lae and Salamaua. A Japanese bomber attacked Port Moresby but did little damage.

While the troops battled heat and humidity in New Guinea, below zero temperatures were forecast in New York City, and the city was nearly out of heating oil[45].

THURSDAY, 14 JANUARY, 1943: Charlie didn't say much on this date due to censorship, except that he was gaining weight. In New Guinea, A-20s strafed the Labu area and small boats in Sachsen Bay. B-25s bombed the fuel dump and other supplies along the beach in the vicinity of Voco Point near Lae. B-24s carried out attacks on Madang and Finschhafen, and also bombed Gasmata Island.

Women were playing a more active role in supporting the war effort. The Curtis-Wright Company sponsored a plan to train college women to fill engineering positions in its plants. About 400 women enrolled as "cadettes" in classes to open February 1 at Rensselaer Polytechnic Institute in Troy, NY[46].

FRIDAY, 15 JANUARY, 1943: US troops enveloped pockets along the Soputa-Sanananda road. The bombers continued their support of the ground forces; A-20s attacked the Sanananda Point area as B-25s bombed supply dumps at Lae; B-24s bombed bridge construction at Wewak. In the Bismarck Archipelago, B-24s hit the airfield on Gasmata Island and carried out assaults on the runway at Cape Gloucester, New Britain Island. Major Kenneth D. McCullar took over command of the 64th Bomb Squadron.

The movie Saving Private Ryan was loosely based on the fate of the Sullivan brothers, chronicling the effort to save one of several brothers in combat, so that at least he can survive[47]. Sadie will invoke the "Sullivans" later in her efforts to get Ben out of combat once Charlie goes missing. In Waterloo, Iowa, Mrs. Thomas F. Sullivan had no reason to hope that any of her five sons had survived the sinking of the Juneau in the South Pacific. The Navy had notified her that her sons were MIA, but a survivor of the Juneau sinking wrote to say he saw one son, George, die on the life raft he was on, and that the other four went down

with the ship. The Sullivan boys were George, 29; Francis, 26; Joseph, 23; Madison, 22; and Albert, 20[48].

SATURDAY, 16 JANUARY, 1943: Charlie was in an Officers' Club somewhere in Australia. He wired money home because there was "no place to spend it." The airmen employed A-20s to attack the Soputa-Sanananda trail, the Kurenada area, and the area south of the Kumusi River. US and Australian ground forces assaulted Sanananda, which fell the next day. B-25s again bombed supplies at Lae. B-24s attacked airfields at Gasmata Island; the town of Finschhafen, New Guinea; and a cruiser east-southeast of Cape Orford.

I wonder had Sadie been 20 years younger, if she would have been more active in service. Opportunities were certainly opening up for women. In another sign of the times, Ensign Loraine Cornelisen became the first woman officer to enter the Brooklyn Navy Yard in its 141-year history. Ensign Cornelisen was a member of the first graduating class of WAVEs (Women Accepted for Voluntary Emergency Service) and she attended Mount Holyoke College. Her arrival broke a longstanding "no women" tradition at the Yard. Fifteen hundred other women workers also came on board. Furthermore, the Army agreed to grant military status to women serving as dietitians and physical therapists[49].

SUNDAY, 17 JANUARY, 1943: The battle intensified in New Guinea, A-20s strafed Mambare Delta and hit positions between Bakumbari and Salamaua. B-25s again bombed supply stores at Lae. B-24s attacked Finschhafen and Madang wharf areas, Malahang Airfield, and a vessel southeast of Rambutyo Island. B-17s bombed landing grounds and disrupted shipping in Rabaul. B-24s attacked the airfield on Gasmata Island. Three American B-17s on the ground were destroyed when Japanese planes bombed Milne Bay. No ground personnel were injured.

While these airmen were fighting and dying, Horace J. Haase, 34, prominent in the Brooklyn chapter of the America First Committee, was arrested as a violator of the Selective Service Act. Since March 1942, Haase had led "Americans for Peace." America provoked the Japanese attack, Haase maintained, and furthermore, Germany and Japan were on the right side[50]. In 2016 a presidential candidate used "America First" as a campaign slogan. I doubt that Mr. Trump was intentionally linking his campaign to the earlier, sometimes pro-Nazi organization. However, "America First" is a tainted phrase. President Trump continued to use it.

MONDAY, 18 JANUARY, 1943: Charlie, still had not received a letter from home, and he wondered if Ben had enlisted yet. B-25s attacked a motor pool and supply dumps at Lae, as planes bombed Madang and Malahang Airfields and attacked a cargo ship southeast of Rambutyo Island.

We take for granted today that the Air Force is a separate branch of the military. In 1943, The US House of Representatives planned to consider a resolution by Carl Vinson (D. GA) to unite the US Army and Navy Air Forces. Representative Vinson had a long career supporting a strong military, was responsible for the "two ocean" Navy, and was chairman of the House Naval Affairs Committee[51].

TUESDAY, 19 JANUARY, 1943: In New Guinea the fighting expanded as A-20s strafed troops in the Kurenada area; B-25s hit barracks areas and supply dumps at Toeal and pounded supply dumps at Lae. Heavy bombers attacked targets at Lae, Madang, Cape Hollman, Cape Saint George, Finschhafen and Gasmata Island.

Charlie wrote an, "I'm fine" letter to Sadie during a time he was recuperating from wounds suffered in combat. On December 9, Edward J. Hedberg of Brooklyn wrote to his mother that he was feeling fine and did NOT mention that he was wounded in action on November 13. Mrs. Hedberg learned of her son's injuries from a government telegram received on New Year's Day. The younger Hedberg, a gunner on the Atlanta, was hurt when the ship went down near the Solomon Islands. Hedberg's father Vincent, veteran of the First World War, was a policeman in Coney Island[52].

WEDNESDAY, 20 JANUARY, 1943: When Charlie's squadron was on the way to Port Moresby, he managed to send two money orders home just before shipping out. The bulk of his unit's B-25s bombed supply dumps at Lae and targets on Aroe Island, as B-24s attacked Madang and Finschhafen as well as Cape Gloucester, New Britain Island, and Gasmata Island. The 64th and 65th Bombardment Squadron (Heavy), 43rd Bombardment Group (Heavy) with B-17s transferred from Mareeba, Queensland, Australia to Port Moresby, New Guinea.

The US was fighting a world war and the need for soldiers was great. Thus the government announced that it was dropping the age of enlistment from 18 to 17[53].

THURSDAY, 21 JANUARY, 1943: The Fifth Air Force continued to add resources and thus ramped up their attacks in the New Guinea area. B-17s bombed the airfield and shipping in Rabaul, while in northeastern New Guinea, B-25s hit supply dumps and airfields. Meanwhile in Dutch New Guinea a B-24 attacked a cruiser at Amboinea harbor on Ambon Island. Japanese ships in Simpson Harbor, Rabaul, were on the receiving end of skip bombing attacks from B-17s with concomitant improvement of the hit rate from the American attackers.

Charlie (and later Ben) communicated with their family via air mail and the cheaper method using "V mail," short for Victory mail. V mail was a censored and thus a secure means of communication. A mother with a son fighting overseas wrote from Brooklyn to the government complaining that her only means of communicating with her son was V mail[54], which was censored and copied. Many of the letters I have from Charlie, Ben, and Sadie are V-mail. Here is an example.

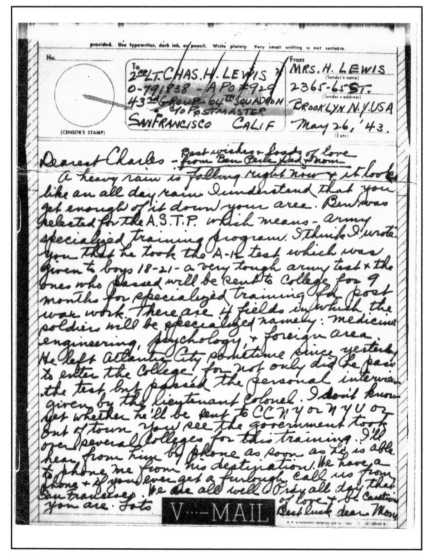

FRIDAY, 22 JANUARY, 1943: The Papua Campaign ended with the collapse of organized resistance by the Japanese on the Sanananda front. Allied forces secured the air base at Dobodura on the north side of New Guinea, which would become a major source of Allied air operations. Missions leaving from Dobodura negated the need to fly over the Owen Stanley Mountains to reach Rabaul. The battle against the Japanese in Rabaul continued as B-24s bombed Simpson Harbor and shipping and searchlights at Rabaul. In the Dutch East Indies B-24s attacked a vessel off Ambon Island. B-25s bombed Lae Terrace; A-20s strafed small boats in Baden Bay and at Woiba Island.

Charlie was fighting to defend freedom, yet incidents like this one in Brooklyn still happened: After Temple Ahavath on Quincy Street was vandalized, the local police captain refused to post an officer for Saturday services, telling the Rabbi, "to keep the thing quiet, it'll all blow over[55]."

SATURDAY, 23 JANUARY, 1943: Allied forces split their time between attacking Japanese positions on northern New Guinea and on New Britain. B-17s attacked the airfields at Rabaul and shipping off Cape Gazelle. B-24s attacked transports north of Rabaul and at Simpson Harbor. In New Guinea, B-25s attacked supply dumps in the terrace area of Lae. B-24s hit Madang and Finschhafen.

The aforementioned Brooklyn native Sergeant Meyer S. Levin was to receive a decoration posthumously for his part in the sinking of a Japanese battleship on December 11, 1941. The Army announced 100 more colleges were adding pilot training consistent with the expanding nature of the war[56].

SUNDAY, 24 JANUARY, 1943: The attacks on Rabaul continued. These actions were extremely dangerous because of the ground fire and air assaults the Japanese launched against the Allies. B-17s bombed the airfield, harbor and shipping at Rabaul. B-24s bombed runways at Cape Gloucester and Gasmata Island and B-25s hit supply dumps at Lae.

Pilot 1st Lieutenant Vernon A. Strawser, Jr. and co-pilot Robert Corrie flew a high altitude reconnaissance mission to Rabaul carrying an extra gunner in the nose section instead of a bombardier. Instead of bombs they carried extra fuel. Over Rabaul, enemy fighters attacked Strawser and Corrie's plane, injuring both of them. The Japanese damaged an engine, forcing the plane into a steep dive. The Japanese planes broke off the attack, perhaps believing the B-17 was about to crash. However, the injured Corrie stabilized the plane. The crew decided that Strawser's injuries were so severe that they didn't have time to fly back to Port Moresby. So they landed at Dobodura, becoming the first B-17 to land there. Sadly, Strawser died from his wounds.

The *Brooklyn Eagle* provided "stars of honor," simple 5-pointed silver stars, for family members of men in service to wear on lapels which the Lewis family was eligible to wear.

A Mrs. Fredrick Amour kissed her husband goodbye as he left for his army induction, and there and then decided to join the WAAC (Woman's Army Auxiliary Corps). When Mrs. Armour came home that day, she was surprised to find her husband in the kitchen making dinner. He'd been rejected, while she had been accepted[57].

MONDAY, 25 JANUARY, 1943: The US Air Force focused on northern New Guinea, with A-20s attacking northeastern Papua where enemy movement appeared. B-25s blasted supply dumps and AA and machine gun positions around Lae. B-24s assaulted a beached ship at Finschhafen while planes attacked runways on Gasmata Island and at Cape Gloucester.

The Civil Rights movement was still many years away. The American military was still strictly segregated. The American Civil Liberties Union challenged the constitutionality of draft quotas based on color by appealing the refusal of the Brooklyn Federal Court to grant a writ of Habeas Corpus to Winifred Lynn, a 36-year-old "Negro." The appeal would be the third court contest of Lynn's induction on the grounds of racial discrimination. Lynn originally refused to report for induction on the grounds that the segregation of Negro soldiers in the army violated the Selective Service Act, that "in the selection and training of men for service there shall be no discrimination on account of race or color[58]."

TUESDAY, 26 JANUARY, 1943: Allied flyers split their efforts between Rabaul and New Guinea proper. While B-17s bombed shipping and the Rapopo airstrip in Rabaul, B-24s attacked the runways at Cape Gloucester and Gasmata Island. There were also attacks in the Lae area and Finschhafen. B-17s encountered Japanese night fighters on these missions, a future menace for the Americans.

Families learned that their loved-one was missing in action, holding out hope for a good outcome. Charlie and Ben would both be reported as missing in action. In Brooklyn, Captain William Hickey of the NYC Fire Department still prayed that his son, Fireman Third Class Joseph Thomas Hickey, 22, had survived the sinking of the Juneau (the same ship on which the Sullivan brothers were killed). Alas, young Hickey was one of the fatalities[59].

WEDNESDAY, 27 JANUARY, 1943: The air war in New Guinea continued on as A-20s hit huts and AA positions at Garrison Hill while B-25s pounded the supply storage and runway at Malahang. B-24s bombed Finschhafen town and the runway on the tip of the Huon Peninsula. B-24s bombed the airfield on Gasmata Island.

On this day, Charlie was the navigator on a B-17-F flown from Mareeba, Australia, to Jackson, near Port Moresby. Here is the Officers Club on Port Moresby[60].

From the Officers Club, Port Moresby[60].

Chapter 7

Charlie's First Combat[17]

NOW CHARLIE WAS ON THE GROUND AT PORT MORESBY and was present as the air war continued. On January 28, A-20s bombed the area from Garrison Hill to the Komiatum Track and B-17s hit the Wewak area. B-24s carried out attacks at Salamaua. In the Bismarck Archipelago, B-24s attacked a cargo vessel in Open Bay and a nearby village on New Britain Island. In the Dutch East Indies, B-24s bombed a transport off Ambon Island. Charlie's units were bolstered by the move of HQ 3rd Bombardment Group (Dive) and its 8th Bombardment Squadron (Dive) with A-20s and 90th Bombardment Squadron (Dive) with B-25s from Charters Towers, Australia to Port Moresby.

The B-17 attack in Wewak on January 28 was likely Charlie's first combat mission, piloted by Captain McCullar. Wewak is pretty far up the coast of New Guinea, northwest of Madang. Bruce Gamble, author of "Fortress Rabaul," described what it was like for the crew of a B-17[12]:

> *"Inside the bombers, gunners spun their turrets or pivoted their hand-held weapons back and forth, squeezing bursts, trying to fire ahead of on-rushing Zeros. The interior of a Flying Fortress was all metal-a simple framework of aluminum covered by a thin outer skin-which for the crew was like being on the inside of a giant drum. The entire plane shook from recoil of machine guns, and the pounding gunfire reverberated loudly. Acrid smoke drifted through the fuselage, accompanied by the clatter of hot brass shell casings against the metal floors. The steady throb of the Wright Cyclone engines and the rush of the slipstream through the bomb-bays and gun ports became background noise, punctuated at times by the bang of enemy cannon shells or the eerie zing of deadly shrapnel. Bullets rattled against the outer skin and buzzed through the fuselage with the sound of angry bees. Men cursed and ducked instinctively at the near misses, or grunted softly when their bodies were torn by unseen objects traveling almost the speed of sound."*

The description of combat in a bomber is in contrast to the safe lives that politicians and diplomats were living. The *New York*

Times reported that former ambassador to Russia Joseph E. Davis said it will be "a pushover" to defeat Japan after Hitler is defeated[61]. I don't think Mr. Davis had spent much time in combat.

On Saturday January 30, Charlie's second combat mission attacked the shipping lanes near Rabaul. Charlie's mission on that day began a trend of changing crews and planes on virtually every mission. His pilot, Captain Charles N. McArthur, would be killed on April 17 with the rest of his crew when their B-17 collided mid-air with another plane shortly after takeoff from Port Moresby. And so the next day, Charlie flew his next mission with pilot Lieutenant Robert Schultz, who survived the war.

"Dear Mom, Sorry I haven't been writing more often. Mostly laziness-and the fact that I can think of nothing to say until I hear of something from you," Charlie wrote on February 1. The nonchalant tone belied the fact that he had just completed three bombing missions over Rabaul. Captain Carl A. Nelson piloted the most recent mission, that very day, and he survived the war. A postscript mentioned that Charlie needed cigarettes because he was smoking more than the ration, and he thought his family could mail him a carton for 60 cents. Alas, Charlie, wrote two days later, he couldn't receive packages from home thus…no cigarettes.

On February 3[62], Charlie flew again to New Britain, this time bombing Gasmata. His pilot, Lieutenant James T. Murphy, along with McCullar perfected skip bombing. On February 6, Charlie was part of a massive attack on the Lae Aerodrome, where Australian coast-watchers had reported 60 Japanese planes on the ground. Charlie's pilot was Lieutenant Robert Schultz, who survived the war.

Unfortunately, when the Allied planes arrived at Lae, all the Japanese planes were gone – they were busy attacking the Allied airbase at Wau. When the Allied planes returned, they encountered many of the attacking Japanese bombers and fighters. A fairly large air battle followed, with 25 Japanese aircraft shot down without any Allied losses. Lt. Schultz's crew also spotted two enemy submarines.

On February 14 and 15, Charlie flew with Major McCullar on yet two more bombing runs to Rabaul and back. These missions were part of a raid with 37 American bombers. The Allied planes attacked in two-minute intervals to disrupt air and ground defenses. Given that the Allied Intelligence had partially broken the Japanese code, they had a good idea that the enemy were planning to launch a major convoy from Rabaul to reinforce the Japanese base on Lae. Codebreakers estimated that the Japanese would send upwards of 6000 troops in convoys to Lae.

During the rest of February, the 64th Bomb Squadron attacked the shipping lanes near Rabaul, hoping to disrupt Japanese plans and perhaps strike gold and find the presumed gigantic Japanese convoy. Charlie flew missions on February 19 and 20 piloted by McCullar and Captain Harry A. Staley, respectively. Captain Staley would die in April when McCullar's plane crashed. On the February 19th mission, the plane landed on the northern part of New Guinea to re-fuel and get food for the crew before returning to Port Moresby. A few days earlier, a plane piloted by Lieutenant Niell G. Kirby had run out of fuel and landed on a grass field at Hood Point, and had to await fuel to finish his flight to Port Moresby.

On February 24, with pilot McCullar, Charlie somehow took part in two bombing runs to Rabaul. His message home was cryptic, perhaps attempting to elude the censors:

"For news of what I am doing you would know as much as I do by reading of our exploits in the newspapers. I heard a broadcast from San Francisco which played up one in which we received commendations. Do not be surprised at this since I am with a different outfit now. We use different type of equipment than I trained in the States."

On this mission, Charlie's plane conducted skip bombing. The plane of one of Charlie's future pilots, Captain Ray E. Holsey, sustained serious damage when one of its own bombs detonated too soon, although the plane managed to return to base safely.

After the February 20th raid, the air crews met with American infantry who had been fighting the Japanese in the jungle of New Guinea. Here the airmen learned of the Japanese atrocities. The infantry reported seeing Australian soldiers hanging from trees where they had been used for bayonet practice. Evidence of cannibalism was found on American corpses. American POWs were tied to trees, left to die of thirst or starvation.

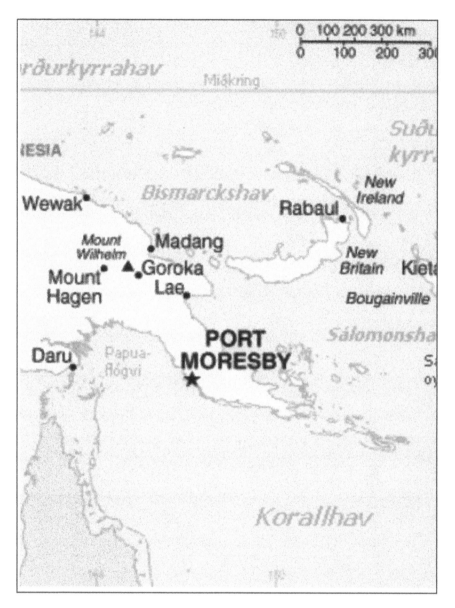

The Bismarck Sea[63].

Chapter 8

Battle of Bismarck Sea-
Silver Star[16,19,21]

THE JAPANESE CONVOY attempting to re-supply Lae from Rabaul (far upper right of the map) faced a choice: go east then south and turn west to Lae (basically a clockwise circle) or go north and then west (counterclockwise) through the Bismarck Sea. The weather was bad over the Bismarck Sea on March 2, 1943, so General Kenney guessed that the Japanese would use this as a cover to go to Lae. He was right. On March 1, a lone B-24 flown by Lieutenant Walter Higgins spotted the convoy en-route to Lae. Higgins had evaded three attacking Japanese fighter planes and ducked into the clouds to get away, spotting the Japanese convoy when he emerged.

Charlie flew what may have been a "recon" mission on March 1, bombing the southern portion of New Britain at Gasmata. On March 2 he flew two combat missions. 64th Bomb Squadron commander Major McCullar piloted the first and Captain Raymond Holsey, the second. Charlie's squadron sank the troop carrier Kyokusei Maru, carrying 1200 men and damaged two other troop carriers, Teiyo Maru and Nojima[64].

The Battle of Bismarck Sea had begun. It would be the first major battle to use skip bombing. Their high success rate hitting their targets no doubt was due to this new but dangerous bombing method.

Magazine photo of 64th Bombardment Squadron pilots in April 1943 (left to right) Captain Ray Holsey, Major Kenneth McCullar, Major Harold Hastings[65].

It was on Charlie's second mission on March 2 that he made history. He described it in some detail in a letter to his brother. The unit history corresponds to events Charlie described and none other than General George Kenney described Charlie's actions in a letter to Sadie:

> *"Second Lieutenant Charles H. Lewis was navigator on a B-17 type aircraft which was one of a formation of eight that attacked the Lae convoy of 14 warships and cargo vessels near Sakor Island on March 2, 1943. The convoy was sighted maneuvering in a large circle with six warships for protection on the outer edge of the circle. Lieutenant Lewis manned the machine guns in the nose of the aircraft against the enemy fighters which were intercepting our aircraft immediately following the bombing run. During this action, Lieutenant Lewis was wounded by 7.7 mm machine gun fire. Notwithstanding his injuries this officer continued his fire against attacking enemy aircraft. He then directed the pilot on his course for the three hundred and fifty mile trip back to the base. Lieutenant Lewis again displayed the courage and fortitude which is making our operations in the Southwest Pacific Area a success."*

Other planes heard the radio chatter between Charlie's pilot Ray Holsey and Charles Giddings piloting a different plane as Charlie returned to base. Gordon Manuel[66] was on one of the planes bombing ships in the Bismarck Sea and recounted the events as well[19,66].

"Jeez! The sky's full of Zeros!" radioed Ray Holsey, the pilot of Charlie's plane. "This is it! Watch your step!" yelled someone else on the plane.

"Charlie!" Holsey radioed, trying to get Giddings' attention.

"Sounds like Ray," said someone on Giddings plane.

"Charlie, I'm on fire! Follow me down, will you? I'm on fire!" yelled Holsey.

Giddings maneuvered the plane to shield the wounded B-17.

"Sure Ray, right above you. Keep your nose up."

"It's sure hot in here," said Holsey.

"Yeah Ray, you ain't kiddin'. Sure does look kinda warm. You look like a kettle on the stove," said Giddings.

Holsey must have thought about ditching his plane, but managed to reach base, the wounded Charles Lewis navigating the plane home safely.

General Kenney didn't mention that Charlie was manning the nose gun because the gunner had been wounded or killed. As navigator, Charlie was in close proximity to the pilot and the nose-gunner and the 7.7 mm round that wounded Charlie was the caliber of the machine gun on the Mitsubishi A6M Zero. Charlie's comment while training in Florida – "Oh yes. Operating a power turret (machine gun) I set the range record for consecutive hits on a moving target the other day. Not my job but handy to know"– was indeed prophetic: He shot down an enemy fighter plane.

In a series of letters Charlie told his version of the battle, but mentioned nothing about his wounds for over a month. In a rare letter that evaded the censors, Charlie wrote on March 7, five days after being injured and perhaps two days after getting out of the hospital,

> *"I am flying a 'flying fortress' now. Have been ever since I came over. I have been on many bombing missions. I can't say where. The other day we destroyed a lot of Jap boats. It was a complete annihilation of their forces. I have no exact figures but we estimate they lost upwards of 20,000 men on their transports- not to mention a whole flock of Zeros."*

In May, Charlie wrote to Ben about his injuries,

> *"Well 'kid' I think I ought to straighten you out about a few facts. I was not in the hospital 28 days. It was 3 days. I was shot by a Zero. Received minor wounds along my leg and thigh. Only good one was in the leg. I still have pieces inside. But it missed all of the vital points and so I was okay. The leg wound healed without a scar (almost) and you'd never know it if I didn't tell you. I was back on flying duties 3 days after I was hit. Also I might mention the Japs are minus one Zero. That is the straight dope. There is more I could say-but censorship you know. Don't tell this to mom of course-except that I am perfectly okay."*

Chapter 9

Communications

"**DEEPLY REGRET TO INFORM YOU YOUR SON** Second Lieutenant Charles H. Lewis Air Corps was seriously wounded in action in Southwest Pacific area March 2. Reports will be forwarded when received." Thus read the telegram Sadie received on March 12 from General Ulio, the Adjutant General.

Charlie hadn't any inkling that his mother knew he was injured, and so his letters home that month continued the boring "I'm fine. Still haven't received any more letters."

On March 12, Ben's 18th birthday, Charlie wrote to Sadie:

"I'm fine. I've received about 6 V-mails from you. None of the other kind. The latest one was dated 2/14. The airmail you sent the same day hasn't come yet. How is Perle getting along in her job? And how is Ben doing (and what) since he decided to wait to be registered? There is very little to tell you about things up here. They are more or less routine. I don't know how much extra money I may be able to send home. It depends on whether I get a vacation in Australia and how much that will cost me. What with the great distances to travel and all it usually costs a young fortune. But after a while up here you are willing to pay that much for a rest. It is very pleasant here-swell bunch of boys–but, of course, there is nothing to do except read- an occasional outdoor movie."

It wasn't until April 4 that Charlie got wind of the fact that folks back home had heard some news about his possible war wounds:

"One of the boys who flies with me told me his folks received a War Department notice that he was injured. Both he and I cut ourselves on a piece of metal in the nose of the plane. Just a scratch. A little iodine and I forgot about it. But because it happened on a flight to a record of it (sic). I hope you don't get some silly notice to the effect that I have been injured. I was in the hospital long enough to find a bottle of iodine or about 2–½ minutes. I am in excellent health-still putting weight on and getting lazier than usual."

On April 6, Sadie received some comforting news from the Adjutant General's Office:

> *"I am pleased to inform you that a report dated March 30, 1943, has been received from the Southwest Pacific area, stating that your son, Second Lieutenant Charles H. Lewis, 0-791838, has been released from the hospital. Should further information be received concerning him, you will be notified immediately. The message of cheer which you forwarded to this office was transmitted to your son on March 31."*

Perhaps the definitive source of what actually happened to Charlie with respect to the extent of his wounds came from the official Air Force hospital admission card prepared by the Surgeon General, Department of the Army 1942-1945. Charlie's "card" confirmed that he was "white/Mexican", and a flight officer. Hospital admission was March 3, but this could be because he was wounded on his second mission on March 2 and probably returned to base after midnight. His injuries were "shell fragments, shell" explosion in the thigh and gluteal regions. More likely, he was hit by a machine gun round rather than "shell fragments." An injury like Charlie's was similar to that of the fictional Forrest Gump[67]. Gump was receiving the Congressional Medal of Honor from President Johnson:

"Where were you wounded, son?"

"I got shot in the butt-ocks."

"I'd like to see that," answered the president with a hint of a smile.

And Forrest pulled down his pants to show him!

Chapter 10

War Crime?

SHORTLY AFTER CHARLIE'S PLANE limped back to base, an incident occurred during the later part of the battle, which Charlie missed. Lieutenant Woodrow Moore's B-17 was hit by enemy fire and at 5000 feet the crew bailed out. Captain James DeWolfe, piloting a different B-17, witnessed four Japanese Zeros swoop down on the helpless airmen from Moore's plane and machine gun them in the water[19].

"Jesus Christ! Look at that! The sons-of-a-bitches," Moore yelled over the loudspeaker. "Let's get every goddam Jap in sight. Go down and shoot their guts out!"

Gordon Manuel[66] described the first hours of the battle: Ground surface fire hit a B-17 and six crew bailed out. With chutes deployed and airmen slowly descending to the sea, Japanese Zeros hiding in the clouds swept down and killed them. The other crews of the 43rd Bomb Group learned of the Japanese attack on the parachuting airmen by radio while it was happening. Many Japanese ships had been hit, dumping hundreds of their sailors into the water.

While Charlie was in the hospital, the American planes returned to base and refueled and re-armed quickly and left Port Moresby to attack the remaining Japanese ships and sailors in the water. "It was all pretty grim. Poor bloody Japs. They couldn't hit back. They were struggling in the water like drowning rats. It was terrible, but it was necessary," said Australian war correspondent Damien Parer. "I feel very crooked about all this blood and guts," he wrote in his diary[19].

Dick Rowe was another Australian in the Battle. "Every time I strafed them, I said to myself, 'there's one less yellow bastard for the RAAF to sweat for.'" Of 15,000 Japanese that started out in the convoy, only 100 made it to shore[19].

Shooting helpless sailors in the sea was a violation of the Geneva Convention[68], but the Japanese did not adhere to those "rules of war." Examples of atrocities the Japanese committed on their captives are countless. For example, on September 5 off the coast of Guadalcanal, Chief Boatswain's Mate Vernon A. Suydam of Sayville, Long Island, jumped from his flaming destroyer after it was hit by enemy torpedoes. Sayville was in the water with several companions when a Japanese cruiser came at them and opened fire, killing most of the Americans in the water. Sayville attempted to save one of the wounded sailors but he died during Sayville's 23 hour swim to shore[69].

The actions of the Japanese would seem to be war crimes considering item 2 of the Convention: *"It is forbidden to kill or injure an enemy who surrenders or who is hors de combat (outside the fight) or persons incapable of performing their ability to wage war."* Others will judge whether the Allied actions in the Battle of the Bismarck Sea were war crimes too.

Chapter 11

Back to War

AFTER THREE DAYS, Charlie was released from the hospital. While he downplayed the severity of his injuries, the fact that he didn't have another mission until March 26, 24 days after being wounded, suggests that he sustained a bit more than a "scratch." His letters home during this time were government-censored and Charlie-censored, continuing to sugarcoat his living conditions with no hints of truth. As usual Charlie's letters discussed how much money he can send home. In one ominous sentence he wrote, "However if I should send anything home remember that I will need some cash to pay my income tax which will be quite high- so don't put every last cent into war bonds. If you need any money I may send for personal necessities, of course do not hesitate to spend it. I mean this. I do not expect you to save all the money for me." Is Charlie starting to doubt that he will come home?

"Have you met any Japs?" Sadie asked in one letter.

"Not face to face, but in the air, close enough to see them and shoot them. Which is as close as I care to come to them for the time being," Charlie replied.

In another letter he writes, "We sleep in tents. But they are pretty comfortable. We have air mattresses, which are all right. Food is just fair. No milk except canned milk for coffee, etc. We recently completed a very nice clubhouse with concrete floors, a bar, and such incidentals. Mosquito nets are a must over here. You'd never get a night's sleep without them. But mosquitoes are not bad in the daytime."

Charlie returned to combat on March 26[70], flying with pilot lieutenant Glenn E. Ream, who'd been Captain Holsey's co-pilot. Charlie's plane took part in a bombing mission in bad weather over the shipping lanes between Wewak and Finschhafen. When General Walker was killed in January, his replacement was Brigadier General Howard K. Ramey[71]. On this same March 26, General Walker had a memorial service in Washington. Alas also on this day, General Ramey's plane disappeared while on a reconnaissance mission, never to be found.

Charlie had one more mission in March on the 30th with his pilot Captain Nelson, they bombed the shipping lanes near Finschhafen. Charlie wouldn't fly again until April 14.

Meanwhile, the New York City newspapers covered mostly the war in Europe and Africa, with the world largely unaware that the Americans had partially broken the Japanese code[72]. The code-breaking led to a significant event in Charlie's area of combat.

Admiral Isoroku Yamamoto[73] was the supreme commander of all Japanese naval operations and the man who led the attacks on Pearl Harbor. On April 3, the code-breakers learned that Yamamoto would move his headquarters to Rabaul. On April 13, they intercepted a message that gave exact details of a trip the admiral would make to a forward area, Balalae, near Bougainville. The decision whether to attack Yamamoto's plane made it all the way to President Roosevelt, who approved the mission. And American fighter planes did indeed shoot down Yamamoto's plane, killing him. But the Americans didn't announce the death for several weeks, to protect the code-breakers.

Charlie flew a combat mission on April 20 [74] with pilot Lieutenant Morley, but no further information on Morley could be found. Charlie's plane took part in an attack near Wewak, Nubia, and Boram airfields as well as the shipping lanes off of Wewak. On the 17th, he wrote home about Decoration Day, when General Kenney awarded him the Purple Heart for the wounds he sustained on March 2. The letter mentioned the Purple Heart and "I have also been recommended for the Silver Star (3rd highest award, only Congressional Medal and Distinguished Service Cross are higher) but have not received word whether or not it was approved."

Chapter 12

"Missing"

APRIL 19 WAS THE FIRST NIGHT OF PASSOVER. My earliest memories are of celebrating the holiday with Sadie, Hyman and Perle's family. I wonder if Charlie had a Seder that year. There was an open air Seder on Guadalcanal[75].

On April 23, Captain Nelson piloted Charlie's B-17. This time, however, the mission wasn't combat. Over the course of three take-offs and landings, Charlie went from Port Moresby to Garbett, then to Archer Field, and finally to Mascot, Australia, near Sydney[76]. Letters cease until May 11. Charlie's records show that he left Australia for Port Moresby on May 4, arriving May 6.

Could he have gotten leave? If so, he would have written about it. Perhaps crews were needed to transport planes? During the time that Charlie left Port Moresby there was little reported activity. Was it a planned lull when crews were being cycled back to Australia for R&R? These days are lost to history. But when Charlie next wrote, he knew that Ben was in the army.

The number of non-combat accidents increased around this time, especially among pilots and crews with more than 300 hours of flying time. In response, the medical staff strongly urged a change in the fatigue rotation for the crews[24]. So it may be that Charlie had leave in Australia. While there he also may have encountered Australian soldiers returning from combat in North Africa. Frequent fights broke out between Australian soldiers and US airmen because the Aussies were not too happy about the "friendships" springing up between US air personnel and the local Australian women[77].

The American and Australian soldiers and airmen had to put their differences aside. Allied planners were expecting a Japanese invasion of the northeast and northwestern parts of Australia[78]. The Japanese had bases in an arc around the northern parts of Australia, with 2000 planes and 200,000 fighting men ready to attack. On May 3[79] the Japanese launched a large raid on Darwin in northern Australia. The Allies admitted that they suffered their biggest losses ever as the result of a Japanese air attack. It isn't known how close Charlie was to this action.

Back home, families of service members captured by the Japanese were dealing with the news that several Allied prisoners had been executed[80]. Of particular concern were the survivors of the April 18, 1942 raid on Tokyo that Jimmy Doolittle commanded in which B-17s were launched from an aircraft carrier[81]. The raid was more symbolic than practical. The crews knew they didn't have enough range to return to the carriers and little actual damage was done on the ground, so the crews had to plan on landing somewhere in China and hope to find friendly troops. Many of the airmen were captured after bailing out over Japan or when their planes landed in Japanese-controlled areas of China. At least one family learned that their son, captured from the Doolittle raid, had been heard on a Japanese radio broadcast–he was alive, for now.

If Charlie heard from Sadie, she might have told him about a 6-week period of mourning declared by the Synagogue Council of America following the Passover observances[82]. The mourning period was in remembrance of the 2,000,000 Jews exterminated by the Nazis. Jews were being asked to partially fast on Mondays and Thursdays, to make donations to the United Jewish Appeal, and to limit occasions of amusement.

In Poland, the Jews in the Warsaw Ghetto were battling Nazi SS sent to exterminate all of them. They fought bravely using makeshift bombs and weapons against overwhelming numbers of German fighters[83].

Official photograph of Charlie receiving the Purple Heart medal from General Kenney.

Chapter 13

Charlie's Last Missions

CHARLIE'S PREVIOUS COMBAT MISSION was on April 20. After returning from Australia, his next "mission" was not actually a combat mission. The Allies established an air base at Dobodura, on the north side of New Guinea, in May 1943 to eliminate the need for the treacherous climb over the Owen Stanley Mountains. To attack Rabaul from Dobodura was a straight eastern shot over the Bismarck Sea. Charlie was on one of six B-17s that transferred from Port Moresby to Dobodura. However, he flew back to Port Moresby on May 22. Perhaps his mission was to transport supplies or crew members to Dobodura. On May 28, he flew his only mission in a B-24. Multiple B-17 and B-24 bombers attacked Wewak, Dagua, and Boram airfields as well as the coastal road from Wewak to Dagua. The next day Charlie flew a B-17 again, and he safely returned from that mission.

Charlie had flown more than 20 combat missions and various non-combat flights, but the official records list fewer. The discrepancy is unclear. Perhaps the official records defined "mission" differently than did Charlie's notes.

As navigator, Charlie must have always been under stress to keep the plane on course, not crashing into a mountain or dropping into the sea. Conditions in general were very poor for the crews in Port Moresby. Major James King, 43rd Flight Surgeon, reported that after 100 to 130 combat hours, crews suffered a loss of "zest." The airmen experienced mental, emotional, and physical fatigue. The doctor noted changes in personality that were not helped by the primitive living conditions and lousy food. Pilot Ralph DeLouch described the stress succinctly: "crews simply disappeared, they just went out and that was the end of it[12]."

Charlie's personality seemed to be changing, at least based on his correspondence. He was hardly ever testy, but on May 18, apparently responding to pestering from his mother, he wrote,

"About this girl you mentioned-she wrote me and told me you had called her and she was going to visit you. May I point out that I never met the girl etc., etc. – and I do not want you writing and telling me she is nice or otherwise. I am having enough trouble maintaining my correspondence as it is. I think I have to write to someone in almost every state in the Union and I don't know if I will keep up my correspondence with her. I also get about a letter a month from girls I don't know which I never answer. Don't get angry-but I wouldn't want you to feel bad if I stopped writing to this girl."

Three days later, he wrote "Well as you know I am in no mood to write long letters." He had also chastised his sister for not writing more because Perle had written, "Mother has said everything."

Charlie's deteriorating mood was not his biggest worry. More serious danger loomed ahead. He didn't know it, but the Japanese Air Group 251, stationed in Rabaul, was reorganizing [84]. Commander Yasuna Kozono suggested re-working the position of the guns on their fighter planes. Downward-angled and upward-angled automatic cannons would allow the fighters to attack American bombers from above and below. After much discussion, three T1N1 fighters were outfitted with four type 99 twenty mm cannons, two angled downward and two angled upward. The modifications were completed in April 1943. After a month of testing using two captured B-17s, the Japanese used the modified fighters in combat on May 21.

Japanese Flight Petty Officer Shigetoshi Kudo took off from Rabaul at about 3 AM on May 21 under a full moon that enabled him to see the silhouette of American B-17 Honi Kuh Okole (Hawaiian for "Kiss My Ass"), flown by Major Paul I. Williams. Kudo's plane was outfitted with the modifications Kozono had recommended, and he shot down the American plane. Only two crew members, Lieutenant John S. Rippy and Master Sergeant (bombardier) Gordon R. Manuel, parachuted to safety; the rest were killed in the crash. Rippy parachuted into St. George's Channel and swam for hours to reach shore. He was captured and executed in November 1943[66]. Sergeant Manuel also swam to shore, where local people helped him evade capture. Later he joined Australian coast-watchers and met up with other downed aviators. The USS Gato rescued Manuel on February 5, 1944, and he returned to duty.

From Pacific Wrecks.com, Flight Petty Officer Shigetoshi Kudo[85].

After shooting down the Honi Kuh Okole, Kudo spotted a second B-17, but couldn't get off a shot. Then he located a third plane, piloted by Joseph W. Geddes[65], and he shot it down. Five of the crew bailed, but one was injured and captured and immediately killed. The Japanese executed the other four, Lieutenant Leslie W. Neuman, Staff Sergeant Ernest W. Burnside, Corporal John J. Mulligan, and Private Robert E. George. It was November 25, 1943.

Combat missions were dangerous, but so were non-combat missions. Reconnaissance missions faced the same dangers posed by navigation and weather as any combat flight. Furthermore, even though the recon mission didn't have a combat objective, the plane was still flying into unfriendly territory. Here are just some results from reconnaissance missions in May 1943[16].

- Herbert O. Derr's plane returned to base because of engine trouble.

- James C. Dieffenderfer's plane returned after dropping bombs with a malfunctioning gun turret.
- Lieutenant Everett C. Sunderman's plane had to fight off three enemy fighter planes. Although Sunderman's plane was badly damaged and he was injured, the plane managed to return safely to Dobodura.

Captain Byron L. Heichel flew a recon mission. His plane was returning to base when fourteen Japanese fighter planes attacked. When a long aerial battle destroyed three of the four engines, the crew decided to land on the shores of New Ireland, but protruding belly turret guns broke the fuselage upon landing. The aircrew found all but three of their comrades. A local plantation manager later found the dead airmen and properly buried them. Most of those who made it to shore were injured.

Natives met Heichel's crew as they waded ashore and tended to the airmen's injuries. The same local German plantation manager who had buried the three men, Rudolf Diercke, sent a note to the crew in English urging them to surrender, saying the Japanese would treat them fairly. But two members of the crew, Sergeant John E. Fritz and Private Frank L. Kurisko, were executed along with other Allied prisoners near Rabaul on November 25, 1943. Japanese took the plane's navigator, Lieutenant Marcus L. Mangett, to an infirmary, but he was never seen again.

Captain Heichel endured terrible treatment by his Japanese captors. The Japanese soldiers flicked their bayonets at a bone fragment protruding from Heichel's nose. Guards beat him for days, only feeding him after five days of captivity. After more beatings and interrogations, the Japanese flew Heichel to Rabaul, where he was reunited with several members of his crew, but learned that Sergeant Kenneth P. Vetter was left to die tied to a wooden post. Some crew members and civilian prisoners tended to Heichel's injuries.

After two weeks on Rabaul, Heichel and three other crew members, Sergeant James E. Etheridge, co-pilot Lieutenant Berry T. Rucks, and Sergeant Clarence G. Surrett, were placed on a boat bound for Japan. All four ended up in Ofuna Prison, and were held at the same time as Louis Zamperini of US Olympic team fame. They all survived, despite brutal conditions and slave labor.

As flight surgeon Major King noted, the crew left for a mission and then came back to find that some of their mates were gone. Just gone. Rarely to be seen again. So it was under this stress and these conditions that Charlie wrote his last letter home:

> *"Dear Mom,*
>
> *I am fine. I guess I was short tempered in some of my last letters. But there were reasons for that I cannot discuss here. You've just got to remember that things do not always run smoothly for us.*
>
> *Well I can't think of anything else to say. So give my love to all.*
> *Love, Charles"*

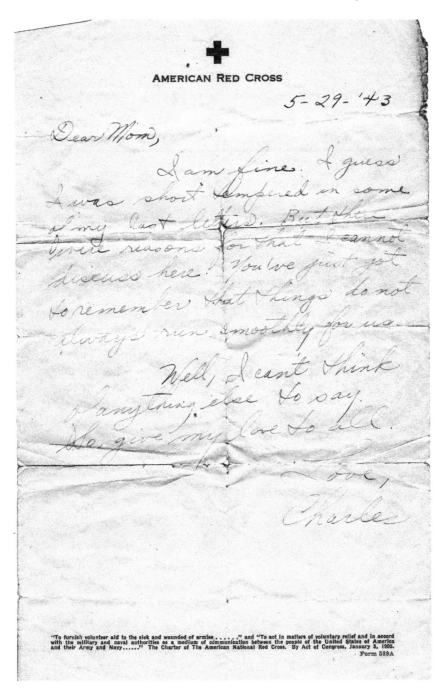

Charlie's last letter.

On June 1, a lone B-17 left Port Moresby on a reconnaissance mission to Rabaul with its crew:

1st Lt. Ernest Nauman, Pilot, Baldwin, NY

2nd Lt. Winslow G. Gardner, Co-pilot, Ogden, Utah

2nd Lt. Charles H. Lewis, Navigator, Brooklyn, NY

2nd Lt. Oliver R. Alvin, Bombardier, North Branch, MN

TSgt. Thomas H. Fox, Aerial Engineer, Mechanicville, NY

SSgt. Paul J. Cascio, Armorer, Baltimore MD

SSgt. Virgil E. DeVoss, Armorer, Danville, IL

Sgt. Bruno B. Bukalski, Armorer, Kouts, IN

Sgt. Albert Smith, Radio Operator, Philadelphia, PA

Sgt. Charles H. Green, Armorer, Morgantown, WV

Their plane, B-17E #41-9207, "Flagship of Texas," #6, did not return to base.

Charlie and his crew-mates made the ultimate sacrifice for their country. New York State Senator Martin J. Kennedy was a World War I veteran who knew something about serving one's country. He spoke to a large crowd in New York City for Memorial Day observances in 1943. Kennedy added four responsibilities to FDR's famous Four Freedoms. "If we would preserve for our posterity those privileges of a free people, then we must equally assume four Responsibilities: For the freedom of speech, responsibility of patriotism, freedom from fear, the responsibility of service, freedom from want, the responsibility of charity and sacrifice, freedom of worship, the responsibility of tolerance[86]."

Chapter 14

Ben's Training in the States

MY FATHER, BENJAMIN LEWIS, turned 18 on March 12, 1943. He graduated Lafayette High School in Brooklyn and briefly attended City College. He enlisted in the Army immediately after his birthday that year, and on April 12, he received the, "Memorandum to enlisted Man Being Called to Duty."

1. Report to the Railway Transportation Officer, Store Number 7, Lower Level Pennsylvania Station, New York City

2. The number 0800 is 8:00 A.M. of the morning of your effective date of call to active duty.

3. Only the minimum amount of clothing are to be taken for approximately three days.

4. All enlisted reservists formerly on active duty will bring with them all items of Government Issue clothing and equipment which they retained when relieved from active duty.

You are in the Army now so make sure you know "0800" is 8:00 AM!

Ben was processed at Camp Upton, which is roughly the location of today's Brookhaven National Laboratory in Suffolk County on Long Island. I spent a summer working at the lab and can verify that many of the buildings look like army barracks. Another family personal note: My wife's grandparents met at Camp Upton circa 1917 while her soldier grandfather, Sam Aaronson, was recovering from the flu and his future wife, a nurse, tended to him.

Ben immediately went to Camp Carson, Colorado, for basic training. He wasn't as diligent a writer as his brother, but he did inform his mother that he was likely to pull KP (Kitchen Patrol) on Sunday. Apparently either Sadie or Perle considered coming out to visit him. At that time, Charlie was way off in New Guinea. Like his brother, Ben arranged for much of his pay to be sent home and he bought an insurance policy.

Ben had to adjust to army life:

"The food here is swell and I'm learning to eat everything since if you leave too much over they put you on KP as a <u>punishment </u>but so far I haven't been punished. Until next Sunday or Monday, I'm restricted to the hotel after hours. But next week I have to recite the "General Orders" by heart in front of a Sarge and get a pass which allows me out every night after 4:30 and Sundays unless I get some special duty."

During April, Ben completed basic training and took a number of tests. One was to enter the ASTP (Army Specialized Training

Program[87]), established in December 1942 to identify, train, and educate academically-talented enlisted men as a specialized corps of officers during World War II. Utilizing major colleges and universities across the country, the Army provided a four-year college education plus specialized technical training for one and one-half years to selected enlisted men.

The men of the ASTP wore the octagon shoulder patch insignia of the program on their uniforms (shown). It depicted the lamp of knowledge crossed with the sword of valor – an allusion to both the mental and physical capabilities of these specialized officers-in-training.

Ben's acceptance into the ASTP was essentially dodging a bullet, he wrote to his mother on May 3.

> *"What I say now I'd like you to keep secret between you and I. A lot of the old members of the company are shipping overseas now (26 to be exact) and will continue to move out in the next 60 days. They also told some of the boys that we new men (ASTP boys) would take advanced training for 45 weeks and might make ratings. They would also use us to train the new men to come in the future. So keep this under your hat mom and keep in mind that changes can take place very fast in the army."*

So rather than shipping overseas, he was off to college!

On May 18, Ben received official confirmation that he was accepted to ASTP, and six days later he was pretty sure he'd be going to college in New York City. Probably City College, he thought, but that wasn't to be. He ended up at Fordham University.

So instead of Sadie and Perle visiting Ben in Colorado, Ben was on a train heading back east. Meanwhile, Ben reported that a New York City-bound train was wrecked and 14 people killed and many injured. A fellow in Ben's group found that his mother was killed on that train. Many others were wondering about the fates of relatives and sweethearts.

Ben heard from a childhood friend, Sasha Gilien.

> *"For one, I have my career already mapped out. I'm going to be a writer (of course) for the entertainment world. I met quite a few big men in that line, and nothing would suit me better. Also, one of my truest friends (and, incidentally, my collaborator), Lincoln Haynes, who is a 4f just got a job at Warner's studio, and we have made a solemn pact that when I get out of this nightmare, we shall get together and really turn stuff out."*

Amazingly, Sasha's plan worked and he went on to achieve some notoriety. He became a successful writer, penning "The Big Valley" and "Hawaii Five-0," and was the 11th person in history to get a heart transplant, in 1969, and died two years later.

I have one of Ben's report cards from Fordham University and later obtained the transcript of his three semesters there. Sasha confirmed in his letter to Ben that Ben would attend Fordham University. Sasha, who was beginning Marine officer candidate school, reminisced about growing up with Ben and Charlie:

"I also heard about your brother Charlie and I can imagine how your family is taking it. It is my heartfelt hope tho, that you all will feel, as I do, that he will come back safe and sound, and by everything that is just, he should. As I write, many poignant memories in which Charlie is the center come to me. How he used to teach us...play with us... kid us...argue...show us tricks. All these, and how really a great guy he is..."

The story goes dark until March of 1944, and during this time Ben attended Fordham. His final semester at Fordham ended late March of 1944. Ben likely lived at home and took the subway to class, so there is no letter trail during this time. Ben definitely got his Dad's math gene, scoring his best grades (over 90) in his math classes. He also excelled in English, a skill that would serve him well in his future career as a lawyer. Sadly for me, a retired chemist, Ben's lowest grades were in chemistry.

Due to the impending invasion of Normandy and the shortage of manpower, the army disbanded the ASTP in spring 1944. Ben was a member of the 104th Timberwolf Division, which trained in Colorado Springs. So when ASTP went away, Ben received his travel papers to re-join the active military and arrived in Colorado on March 31.

In the book "Terrible Terry Allen [88]" another ASTPer at Fordham, Bill McIlvaine, described arriving in Camp Carson and hearing General Terry Allen speak to the new Timberwolves. General Allen was a veteran of WWI and of both the North Africa and Sicily campaigns in WWII until being reassigned to lead the

104th. Allen clashed with all of his superiors, including Generals Eisenhower, Bradley, and Patton, but was well liked by his troops. He insisted on rigorous training and worked hard to keep his men properly supplied. Terry Allen was a strong believer in night operations, thinking that the attacking force had an advantage then. At the end of his time in Sicily Allen wrote, "Excessive casualties are the exception in a well-disciplined unit that has been trained to react instinctively under any emergency."

Sadie and Ben just before he left for his second at tour of Camp Carson.

A letter from Ben describing his train trip from New York City to Camp Carson revealed that he went through money faster than did his brother.

> *"We left N.Y.C at 10:45 A.M. Tues. March 28. We went to Albany then Buffalo under (sic) Lake Erie & then thru Ohio, Indiana, Ill., Missouri, Kansas, Nebraska & finally Colorado. The trip took 3 days and boy am I really tired out so I won't make this too long a letter. However I'll write you about all the details about the place over the weekend and mail it air-mail as I will mail all my mail at first. I didn't receive that money order yet and I'm kind of broke, see if you can get about $10 or $20 bucks here I would deeply appreciate it."*

One can imagine the "reception" the regular troops held in Colorado to welcome hundreds of college boys into their ranks. "I was instructing the new men on the workings of the 57 mm gun today. They are all from the ASTP and they are sharp as a tack but I would have kicked them in the teeth. They think they are better than us infantry men. These new recruits are just out of college and they take basic training in the morning and we teach them in the afternoon," wrote Charles H. Norris in "Life in the Army, Letters to Jean[89]." Norris was an original Timberwolf, joining the division when they were stationed in Camp Adair Oregon and moving to the Arizona-California desert and finally to Camp Carson. But not all the new recruits sensed the frustration of their instructors, "I felt I was welcomed into B Company and made to feel like a fellow

Timberwolf very quickly," wrote another veteran of ASTP who ended up in the 104th [88].

The "elephant in the room" during training was that a soldier's job is to kill. Ben addressed it in a letter home:

> *"The really only tough part of it is trying to learn to kill. For instance one Lt. spoke to us on the psychology of war. He told us that it was against American Soldiers because they really don't hate the enemy and that they feared the thought of killing somebody more than anything else. There's a lot in what he says. I still can't see myself killing anybody. In fact we were assured that it would be at least 6 months before anything does happen. So don't worry. I'll be okay in any event."*

Recall that Sadie tried to go behind Charlie's back to get him out of the Army. Well, she was at it again with Ben. Ben referred to Sadie's tactics in two letters. April 13:

> *"So please don't start any campaigns to get me out of the Infantry. There are 10,000,000 men in the service you can see what would happen if every man tried to duck his responsibility. If you want to argue the point wait until my furlough and we'll have about 10 days together to slash the matter out."*

He continued on April 16:

"So don't write to any Congressmen or Presidents about me. I really don't want you to do so. There's a war to win. And someone must do it. Anyway it will be a long time before I go overseas and if I do I won't see any combat for a long time after that."

Ben mentioned that he might have trouble writing because of "night duty," which arose from General Allen's tactic of nighttime attacks. John Light, another ASTP in Ben's 415th Infantry Regiment[91], wrote that they'd typically train until 11 PM or stay out all night on "problems," or military exercises: 10-mile forced marches, practicing night combat, and learning how to attack a concrete pillbox. One such session lasted four days. In another exercise using live ammunition, the troops marched up a steep incline and shot mock pop-up enemies. In squad-sized operations the men had to improvise finding cover and shooting at pop-up enemies from 30 yards away.

Training was proceeding well. Ben achieved "marksman" level – I have his badge, which looks like the one shown. I was visiting the New York State Museum library in Albany, New York, and stopped at a small World War II memorial. This photo of the marksman badge and accompanying poem explain a bit about what it is to be an infantryman.

On May 8 Ben wrote to discuss a furlough, which half the division took at a time. This furlough wouldn't be his last before shipping overseas, but would be his most important one.

Sadie sent Ben $50 so he could get a round trip ticket home when his furlough finally came through. But Ben needed extra spending money because he was trying to see as many of the sites as possible, including Pikes Peak, Colorado Springs, and Manitou, and he wanted to visit a cousin in Denver. But life wasn't all fun and travel. Ten- and five- day maneuvers were coming up; much of this training was night exercises.

The Badge of Glory

Of all the medals upon our chests
From battles and wars we knew,
The one admired as the very best,
Is the one of infantry blue.

It's only a rifle upon a wreath,
So why should it mean so much?
It is what it took to earn it,
That gives it that touch.

To earn this special accolade,
You faced the enemy's fire.
Whether you survived or not,
God dialed that one desire.

For those of us who served the cause,
And brought this nation glory,
It's the Combat Infantrymen's Badge
That really tells the story.
–Author Unknown

Monument in front of NY State Museum, Albany, NY.

June 15 was Infantry Day at Camp Carson. The entire 104th marched past reviewing stands festooned with top brass, including General Allen, but Ben didn't seem too excited about this event.[91]

Ben had some loose ends to tie up before visiting home. He wrote about his "allotment." Like his brother he worried about sending money home, mentioning a 20 percent raise if and when he shipped overseas. After deductions, the family would keep $25 per month and Ben would have $15 for himself – enough.

Ben was also getting his personal life in order ahead of his trip home.

"I got a letter from Sylvia and she is doing well. She can climb the subway stairs now. I'll have to write to her since it is over a week with Sylvia. I wrote to her telling her that it would be better if we 'cooled off' on our romance. The only thing wrong with that she won't cool and insists that I'm the only fellow in her life and no matter what I do she'll never change her mind about me. But it's nothing new to me this business so I'm not worrying about it."

It's a good thing he cleared the decks in the romance department just then, because while home on the long-awaited furlough at the end of June, he met my mother, Edith Weil, at the beach. They saw each other for only a few days, but would correspond throughout the war. Edith's parents, Joseph and Bessie, and Ben's parents met many times and exchanged Ben's letters.

On July 9, Ben was back to Camp Carson. His letters to Edith cover three time periods: Nearly daily from Colorado from June through August 1944; from overseas; and after he returned to the States. Personal details of their letters will remain forever sealed. Suffice it to say, Ben and Edith fell in love on that beach and that love continued until the day my father died, January 31, 1993.

Edith Weil and Ben Lewis, June, 1944.

Rumors flew in Camp Carson about what would become of the 104th. On D-Day, June 6, the Allies had invaded Normandy, fighting a slow campaign stymied by the impenetrable hedgerows that divided the properties and farms in that area of France. But by summer, the Allies had begun to make steady progress taking back France from the Germans. By July 20, Ben felt that orders would come soon. In a letter dated July 21 to Sadie, Ben mentioned for the first time, hearing from Edith. On July 22 he wrote to his mother not to worry, that his unit was slated for "Army of Occupation," which if true was a relatively safe assignment. By August 9 though he still had no word on plans, but he mentioned two letters from Edith, joking that this one might be serious!

In a letter to Edith, Ben mentioned losing his PFC stripe following an argument with an officer, but there was no official demotion letter and Ben was listed as "PFC" going forward, so this incident did not seem too important. On a more positive note, Ben reported taking (and later passing) the grueling test to become "Expert Infantry." The test was initially set up at Fort Benning, GA for the 100th Division and consisted of three days of testing[92]:

To achieve Expert Infantry rating:

- Qualify with one individual weapon and in transition firing; or
- Qualify with one crew-served weapon.
- Complete familiarization firing with one other weapon.
- Complete continuous (without falling out) foot marches, with full field equipment of 25 miles in 8 hours and 9 miles in 2 hours.
- Complete physical fitness.
- Complete the infiltration, close combat, and combat-in-cities courses.
- Qualify in the grenade course.
- Military subject test, evaluated by a board of officers.

The Expert Infantryman Badge, often referred to as the "EIB" is unique among skill qualification badges. The distinctive award, an infantry musket in silver on a rectangular blue background with a silver border, is among the most highly prized peacetime decorations. It can only be earned by an infantryman. It sets him apart–not only as an infantry soldier, but as a soldier who knows his infantry subject matter. You don't have to ask whether he knows his job–you just look at the badge topping the ribbons on his chest.

In 1944 if you were heading east by train you could not communicate. Letters could not find you. There were no phones. August 12 would be the last day Ben could receive mail in Colorado because his division was expected to ship out east. Maybe he'd use his lost house key, which he'd recently found, to surprise everyone before he headed overseas.

In his next letter, dated August 30, Ben was on a ship heading to France. On August 15 General Kenney had received orders to move his division by rail to Camp Kilmer, NJ, with final assembly August 24. The trains took three days to arrive in New Jersey. At Camp Kilmer all the soldiers received immunizations, haircuts, and brief leaves. My mother never forgave Sadie for not telling her that Ben was home for a few days in late August–Edith didn't get to say goodbye. She was visiting relatives in Liberty, NY at the time and most likely couldn't have made it to New York City on short notice, but it would have been nice to have known.

Ben and Hyman, August, 1944.

Chapter 15

Combat

BEN WROTE FROM SEA on August 30, but was obviously censored, saying about the boat only that "it floats." His 56-ship convoy departed the New York-New Jersey area, landing in Cherbourg, France on September 7[90]. Ben didn't get seasick, unlike so many of his fellow soldiers, and I never once saw him get sick even on small boats bouncing around Long Island Sound. The soldiers were cramped aboard ship and tried to go topside as often as they could. Night was pitch black. By day they read, wrote letters, and played cards and dice. Because they reached France in the evening, the official landing did not take place until September 8.·

Rafts ferried the 104th to shore, where the men quickly erected a tent city near the hedgerows and not far from bombed-out villages and treacherously muddy roads. Soon the 104th became part of the so-called Red-Ball Express, a 150-truck army convoy that took over all roads headed east to the front lines. The convoy was necessary because the Allies had advanced so quickly that they out ran their supply lines. So members of the 104th became truck drivers or maintenance men[89]. The Red-Ball Express demonstrated how General Allen cared for his troops. The Army expected all of the trucks to be returned at the end of a particular mission. But General Allen didn't return a single truck, probably thinking that working trucks would be essential once the 104th was in combat. Allen also well knew that the Army famously never delivered requisitioned supplies, especially trucks. So only when a truck broke down or was unusable would he send a truck back to the Army and then request a replacement. Not a single new truck was ever delivered to the 104th from September 1944 until the end of the war[88].

If Ben wasn't a truck driver, he'd have been guarding fuel dumps or prisoners. But his letter home of September 13 didn't reveal much about what he was actually doing, although he asked Sadie to keep in touch with Edith, providing her address.

Ben's letters of September 15 and 19 indicate he was still in France, near where he had landed, but of course censors wouldn't let him say more. He mentioned that towns were off-limits to US GIs, but he must have seen something because he mentioned how hard life was for the civilians. On September 26, the 104th moved east to Barneville, France. They still had relatively safe duty guarding railroads, pipelines, and warehouses, with enough to do so that there was no down time. And General Allen had the troops training around the clock for the combat sure to come. Ben wrote a number of letters over the next few weeks. He knew that Edith and Sadie had met and would do so again, and he was anxious to know about those visits.

On October 7, unbeknownst to Ben, General Allen received the following orders[88]:

"Be prepared to move Division by rail and motor forward on or about Oct. 15. Trucks to carry 6000 infantry with duffel bags. Basic load will have ammunition, gas, oil, repairs and tools. Ship seven rations per man. All vehicles to be fully loaded."

The 104th departed La Haye du Puits, France, with destination Vilvorde, Belgium, just north of Brussels. So beginning on October 16, Ben's unit moved out on a train, "forty and eight," so named because these cars were designed to hold 40 men and eight horses[93]! Ben's last letter home was dated October 13, before his unit entered Belgium and the shooting war.

Ben and his division reached Belgium on October 24. Timberwolf Tracks[90] published a poem by Pfc. Edward J. Apple Jr. describing the train ride there:

SADIE'S BOYS

We read of travel problems now,
and know how those things are;
When civilians rave,
because they crave a streamlined Pullman car.
We sympathize in every way,
when the train's an hour late;
But no doubt the new French system,
would bring things up to date.
It was something like a Pullman car,
that left La Haye du Puits;
And took us to Michelin, from "sunny" Normandy.
A few hundred miles to Belgium,
wasn't going to be so far;
And then they only put just thirty men in every car.
These "sleepers" that they gave us tho',
had all other sleepers beat;
We found as we crawled in the door
and saw-not one damn seat.
And it wasn't quite a normal size,
as we could plainly tell,
But was one thing was for certain-
air conditioning was swell.
The racks were missing from the top,
no fountain at the end;
And the Colonel spoiled the whole damned trip-
"Each car gets ten more men."
We realized-with forty hommes-
what the sign had said was so,
And wondered where the hell they'd put
the missing eight chevaux.
When rations, packs and duffel bags,
and weapons came in too,

We wondered if they'd bitten off-
too much for us to chew.
When some "kill-joy" mentioned sleep just then,
we realized our plight;
And decided that three fourths of us
would spend a sleepless night.
As we hung our packs and helmets
(we felt sure it would work),
Something told us we were moving-
must have been an awful jerk.
We were started on our journey,
now it wouldn't be so bad;
But that little tho't of pleasure,
was the last one we had.
It's funny how soon darkness came-
and without the slightest peep,
Forty men looked all around them,
for a little place to sleep.
As the "looie" crawled into his roll,
spread out upon the floors,
He said, I quote,
"Now you must keep a guard
on both of those doors."
One night!-who were we kidding,
it would take a week, we bet;
After all our night riding,
we weren't off the coastline yet.
Though it seemed we stopped for hours,
one just didn't have to go,
But just get in the position,
and the whistle had to blow.
The dirt collected on our faces-

the beards were doing fine.
Then came the dreaded order,
"Wash and shave by half past nine!"
Oh! Wasn't this all lovely-
so we took the chorus up,
Forty-eight, forty-none and fifty-
shaving in a canteen cup.
When we came to a big city,
we would always draw a crowd.
We were their liberators-
and were we ever proud.
Cigarettes for fifty francs a pack-
was ended just like that.
"Get back in them damn box cars,
AND TAKE OFF THAT WOOL KNIT CAP."
Our pup tents seemed like heaven,
you could set them any place;
Where one could sleep in peace,
without a foot smack on the face.
Where one didn't get a shower,
from the holes up over head,
Or have a helmet hit the "dome,"
just as we got in bed.
We were rugged individuals-
we were on our way to war.
Now we've beaten up the Germans,
and won't ride that way no more.
That's what we tho't till we started
back to the states,
We rode back to France again-hell yes!
In forty-eights.

Forty and Eight Boxcar[93].

Ben was in rifle Company I, 3rd Battalion, 415th Infantry, Colonel John Cochran commanding. The 104th was temporarily assigned to the First Canadian Army. It took many days for the entire division to reach Belgium. While Ben was still in transit, some members of his division were already in combat. Their job was to help open the port of Antwerp to ease supply of the Allies nearing Germany. On October 23, Private Hubert L. Merritt, Company A, 413th Infantry, was the first member of the 104th to be killed in action...there would be more[88,90]. Ben wouldn't write home again until late November, almost five weeks. Clearly he couldn't write while on the train. But then he got very busy.

On October 25, the 104th engaged in their first night combat action. The men sloshed through four foot deep ditches filled with water, carrying their supplies over their heads. When ordered to stop they dug foxholes, two men per hole. One man stood guard from 10 PM to 2 AM and the other until daybreak. While marching at night, the soldiers tied white handkerchiefs on their backpacks so the man behind him could follow in the dark[90].

Ben's company experienced its first small arms fire while taking the town of Heilbloom on the Belgium-Holland border. The first combat went poorly. Many of the men were separated from the main group, and several were taken prisoner. Officers were killed. After the short advance the company retreated to where they'd started. When Company I advanced, they had found Germans well dug in with artillery. Ben's unit attacked a house, from which enemy fire was coming, so the Americans set the house on fire to draw the enemy out. Germans dressed in civilian clothes attempting escape were killed[90].

"Timberwolf Tracks" relates the memories of Private First Class George V. Boyle, who was a member of Ben's 415th Infantry Regiment:

> *"When the Division was first committed to combat the thought that was uppermost in our minds was that this was the test, the final test of our training and ourselves. Questions raced through our minds, 'Will I be able to stand it?' 'Will I be wounded?' 'Will I be killed?' The answer to all these was soon to come. Being a private in a rifle company are (sic) pretty much the same as those of the rest of the men."*

After describing the march, Boyle's memoir continued:

> *"Without any knowledge of having moved I found myself in a ditch listening to shells come whistling in. My first thought was that this was the end and that every shell coming over had my name and address on it. Then I*

began to pray. That didn't last long because in ten seconds all prayers I ever learned became three words, 'God protect me.' The shelling lessened for a few minutes and I got my first idea of what a shell could do to a man. There had been several direct hits on the column and the Medics had taken most of them. I went back to help render first aid. My most lasting impression of my first night of combat was what it is like to have fear."

By October 26 the 104th had re-grouped and with help from British tanks, they moved the Germans out of Belgium and the Americans entered Holland. If you are from Belgium, my father liberated your country.

In "Terrible Terry Allen," Charles Dodd[88], of Company L, 413th Infantry, recalled their first few days of combat. "We dug a foxhole in the middle of the night, settled in and then were ordered to move out." They then marched to the "middle of the war." "I can still hear the medic call out that Sgt. Knorr was dead, shot through the heart…"

The 415th advanced to the Mark River and encountered a storm of German artillery and mortar fire. The fighting on October 26 was particularly bad for Company I, with scores wounded or killed. First Ben's battalion was forced to march through marshy terrain because the actual road was mined. Then they were attacking Germans, who were well hidden in a brickyard. Machine gun fire and at least 20 defenders resisted the company's attack. Mortar fire halted the attack, inflicting additional casualties[90].

Lt. Colonel Gerald C. Kelleher, commander of the third

battalion, ran to the front of the column to rally the troops. Leading the advance, he encountered an enemy patrol of 10 men and, armed with only a pistol, chased them away. He then exposed himself to enemy fire while rescuing his executive officer, carrying him to safety. Colonel Kelleher was awarded the Distinguished Service Cross for his bravery. He also found a stash of documents in Achtenwaal and maps and documents from the Dutch underground. This treasure-trove of papers revealed the entire defense system of the Germans in Holland[88].

Ben was in continuous combat for five weeks from the time he left the train in Belgium. The fighting and conditions were hard. In Holland it was difficult to dig foxholes- the men would always hit water[95]. In some instances, the foxholes were so muddy that the soldiers had to dig "steps" so they could get out without sliding back down into the muck. And although water was everywhere, the men had to use Halazone tabs to purify it enough to drink. Keeping feet dry was impossible, which was why Ben asked for wool socks in many of his letters home. During their entire time in Holland, the troops never slept in a building. And the famous dikes were problematical: they were great for defense (for the Germans), but bad for the attacking troops (the Americans). So many of the American advances were at night because it was easier to surprise the German defenders in the dark.

On October 28, the 415th held the town of Zundert and then advanced on Breda on the Breda-Roosendaal Road. When German artillery attacked at midnight, the Allied artillery drove them back. The advance continued on October 30, when the Americans met up with the 1ˢᵗ Polish Armored Division. The Polish Division, formed in Scotland in 1942, had soldiers who had escaped the German invasion of their country in 1939[96]. Together the Americans and the Poles entered the town of Oudenbosch to wild cheering crowds. "We have been waiting four years, this I should save for you when you come," said an old man as he handed out Dutch chocolate to the soldiers. A little girl asked if the soldiers had seen their princess in America. "Now that we are here, your princess can come home," one GI responded[90].

Also on October 30, the 415ᵗʰ crossed the Mark River in boats, but some were damaged and enemy artillery quickly surrounded several men, cutting them off for three days before they could be rescued. During this time the Americans subsisted on beets and turnips. Even when he was a starving prisoner, Ben traded the despised vegetables for cigarettes. Then the men were stranded in a German-mined beet field. This may have been the event that led to my father avoiding beets during all the years I knew him.

Ben's unit had no time off. They were ordered forward and with British Spitfire air support, took the town of Zevenbergen. On November 5ᵗʰ and 6ᵗʰ, the 415ᵗʰ came to the Maas River near Moerdijk. The Americans went over a dike only to face friendly artillery fire, and had to go up and over it several times under German fire to retrieve their wounded comrades. Finally, when that was over, the Americans had their first hot showers in a month. They re-grouped in Oudenbosch, about to cross an important but invisible line. The 104ᵗʰ was ordered to Aachen–where they would be entering Germany for the first time[88].

As fierce as the fighting in Belgium and Holland had been, the advance into Germany was far more than just a psychological barrier, for the Germans would defend their country to the last man. They built the Siegfried line as a thick, 2-layered defensive wall of cement bunkers, tank defenses, and traps. And November in northern Europe was getting cold!

The goal was to get to the Rhine before the thermometer dipped too low. On November 8th and 9th, the 104th replaced the frontline troops of the 1st Armored Division, also known as The Big Red One. The 1st was General Allen's division before he was removed as their leader in the Sicily campaign. As soldiers of the 104th marched past those of the 1st, they heard murmurs of how lucky they were to have Allen as their general. I doubt my dad felt lucky after all his days in combat.

The first fighting at the Siegfried line was an all-out assault on a heavily-fortified German position on the western edge of Stolberg. Aerial bombing by US and British planes preceded the American attack by land. Ben took part in house-to-house fighting, destroying a German pillbox from a concrete bunker as German machine guns fired on the American troops. Ben was definitely in harm's way.

Back in Brooklyn, Sadie entered the fray.

On November 9, she wrote to none other than Mrs. Eleanor Roosevelt. I only have the response to Sadie's letter from the Brigadier General Edward F. Witsell, acting adjutant general. Sadie's letter mentioned the deaths of all five Sullivan brothers when the USS Juneau sank in the Pacific in 1942. Although the "sole survivor" policy did not go into effect in the army until 1948, the military did grant individual requests from families to remove sons from combat when a previous son or sons were killed in action. Sadie hadn't received any official word about Charlie other than that he was MIA, so she retained a glimmer of hope that her eldest son had survived. But Sadie didn't care about these details; her #1 goal was to get Ben to safety. Her argument: *My older son is missing in action, my only other son is in combat, get him out of there!* She requested that Ben be transferred to non-hazardous duty.

General Witsell replied that a recently announced War Department policy about removing men from combat only applied to families in which two or more sons were MIA or killed and the only surviving son was in the army–not quite the situation in the Lewis family. Ben wasn't coming home.

Right around the time Sadie received General Witsell's response, Ben's company was burrowed into deep foxholes sustaining a 10-hour artillery barrage. On November 16 the Americans entered Aachen, where the GIs attacked the town of Rohe-Herath in a driving, cold rain. They fought in ankle-deep mud and engaged in more house-to-house combat. In four days of action the 415th moved five miles and broke through the Siegfried Line, entering the town of Eschweiler[89]. During the regiment's few days of rest, my father wrote one of his last letters home before his capture:

"Nov. 26, Dear Mom, How is everything this fine and lovely day? I do hope everything is okay. I'm fine and still waiting for the war to end so I can come home to stay. I've even given up the idea of an out-of-town college as I've had enough of this being away. I really appreciated your packages and I could "stand" some more. You can leave out most toilet articles as I have plenty. I could use things like face powder and some hair Vaseline. Also with the increase in cigarette distribution and those on the way I'll have enough for a long time. But things like cookies, candy and wool (heavy) socks I can always use. I receive mail quite regularly now and it's really swell to hear from everyone. Well Mom stay well and give my love to Dad and Perle. All my love Ben."

He wrote to Edith on November 28 and December 1, two days before his capture. Ben clearly figured out a way around censorship. One letter from around this time says "I am in xxxxxx," but also "I am in my fourth country." Since Ben landed in France and fought in Belgium and Holland, he must have been in Germany!

The 104th Division was broken into three regiments; Ben's was the 415th. Generally two regiments were at the front while the third was in reserve, sleeping in a building and getting hot meals. The regiments in turn were divided into Battalions, three rifle and one heavy weapons. Ben was in the 3rd Battalion. Next, battalions were divided into companies with two rifle companies at the front and one in reserve. Ben was in rifle Company I. Unlike a reserve regiment, when a company was on reserve it was always on call and fairly close to the front, so the men didn't get much of a break. The companies were further broken down into platoons and squads.

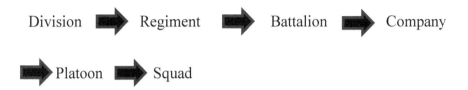

Division ➡ Regiment ➡ Battalion ➡ Company ➡ Platoon ➡ Squad

Back on November 25, the 415th seized the town of Weisweiler. On November 28, Company I relieved Company B near Inden. Company C had to surrender to the Germans due to heavy fighting. The next big engagement would be to take Inden and then on to the factory areas of Lamersdorf and Lucherberg. These two towns were on the east side of the Inde River, which the GIs would have to cross. As usual the attack was to be at night. It would be Ben's last days in combat.

Chapter 16

Capture!

IN 1950, THE FILM "RASHOMON[97]" by director Akira Kurosawa told the story of an "event," a murder and rape, from four points of view. It inspired a classic legal concept, the "Rashomon Effect," referring to eyewitness testimony. Ben's capture had its own slight Rashomon Effect.

In the fighting in Europe, the US Army collected "After Action Reports" based on deposition of combatants shortly after a combat action. What follows are the After Action Reports about the attack of Ben's Company I on the town of Lucherberg. The four sets of accounts largely agree, but differ in some small details. The combined reports paint an extraordinary picture of the events of

December 2 and 3 that lead to Ben's capture. Four sets of interviews relate the actions in Lucherberg on on those days. Sources of information about the attack and capture were:

- 1st Lt. T.E. Danowski, executive officer in charge of the action and 1st Lt. John Thompson, platoon leader, weapons platoon. Both men from 104th Infantry Division, 415th Infantry, Company L, interviewed Dec. 13, 1944.
- Sergeant Leon Marokus, 3rd Platoon, 104th Infantry Division, 415th Infantry, 3rd Battalion Company I, interviewed Dec. 13, 1944.
- Capt. W.H. Buckley, S-3, 104th Infantry Division, 415th Infantry, 3rd Battalion, interviewed Dec. 11, 1944.
- Technical Sergeant T.R. Cheatham, platoon sergeant, second platoon, Sergeant Francis Miller, Communications Sergeant, Sergeant C.F. Shotts, Platoon Guide, 3rd Platoon, PFC D.C. Fleming, Radio Operator and PFC R.J. Vertz, Squad Leader, 1st Platoon, all 104th Infantry Division, 415th Infantry, 3rd Battalion Company I.

The towns nearest Lucherberg, Lamerdorf and Inden, provided little cover. To the south were 800 to 1000 yards of water-filled pits, and to the northwest were two open coal pits on either side of railroad tracks. To the east open fields led to the towns of Pier and Merken. To the west, the direction Company I would attack, a steep hill at the base of a fortified factory area emerged from a 180-foot slag pile.

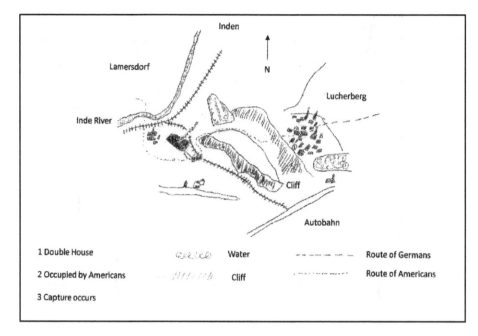

Map of Lucherberg, December 3, 1944.

Just before midnight on December 2, Company I was ordered to attack Lucherberg from Inden, as usual at night. According to the original plan, Companies L and then F would follow. When the moonlight threatened to reveal the GIs, they rubbed dirt over themselves for camouflage. Then when Lieutenant J. J. Olsen led Company I to the railroad bridge over the Inde River, they found the bridge partly destroyed. The men had to cross one at a time, as if tightrope walking, on a single metal rod while hanging on to a metal rod overhead, exposing them to enemy fire and slowing the crossing. Astonishingly, the company made it across the river safely by 0100 hours. Next the men had to cross a marshy area at the base of the cliff shown on the map, at which point the Germans opened fire with small arms.

The German fire prevented the two following companies from crossing, leaving Company I alone to attack the town. Then, under enemy fire, the men ran into a barbed-wire fence. Lieutenant John Shipley ran ahead and then reported that if the Americans could crest the cliff, they could attack and occupy several houses. But Olsen worried about German mortar fire, so he said to the two platoons at the base of the cliff, "I'm making a rush to the town. Stay if you like and stay behind and get wiped out by German artillery[88]." Olsen's men then charged up the cliff into enemy fire and the company burst into the town.

A German tank fired on the men at point-blank range, but withdrew after the Americans returned fire with several bazooka rounds. Then the men entered a house in the northwest part of town. Sergeant Francis Miller led a second group into a double house within an orchard about 100 yards west of a church, and then Lieutenant Olsen took a group into a third house near the church, ordering the men to hold the building.

Yet another group of 10 to 15 men from Company I, likely including Ben, occupied a fourth house, taking 15 prisoners. Olsen was seriously wounded while clearing one house when his gun jammed and an enemy soldier shot him, leaving Lieutenant Edwin Varela in command. The last platoon to reach the town, which included Lieutenants Shipley, Ulmer and Sgt. Marokus, entered the double house (#1 on the map).

While all this was going on, Companies L and F took a long way around to attack from the south to dodge the heavy German fire. Back in Lucherberg, both sides tended to their wounded. The

Americans were low on ammunition but had medics and medical supplies, whereas the Germans had a medical officer but no supplies, my father told me. The Americans were ordered to bring very little ammunition because they'd mostly deploy hand grenades and bayonets.

At 0400 hours Sergeant Marokus, who was fluent in German, helped Lieutenants Shipley, Varela, and Sheridan negotiate a truce with a German medical Lieutenant Colonel so that both sides would "stack their arms," allowing treatment of the wounded to begin. Platoon Sergeant Thomas R. Cheatham and his men got to work. Both sides were following the terms of the truce when a German captain led a group of paratroopers into town and started firing on the Americans. The German medical officer holding a Red Cross flag intercepted the captain and told him about the truce. The shooting stopped, briefly, while the two Germans argued. Marokus pointed out that the German Lt. Colonel outranked the German Captain, and the Lt. Colonel wanted the truce to continue. The German captain decided that a medical officer did NOT outrank him. However, the Captain agreed at 0600 to give the Americans 15 minutes to get out of town.

While the Americans were gathering their belongings and wounded, the Germans began taking them prisoner by ones and twos. The 15 German prisoners in the same house as Ben, started yelling and jumping out windows to rejoin their comrades. When the Germans outside realized Americans were in the house, they quickly entered and took my dad and several others prisoner. All the officers from Company I were killed or captured in this engagement. After the battle, 22 men were listed as missing in action. Ben Lewis was one of them.

Elroy DeMaria was captured with my father and gave his version to a Florida newspaper in 2010[98]. His description of events in Lucherberg match the other reports. On the nights of December 2-3, platoon sergeant DeMaria led 25 men, likely including my father, to one of the houses. Earlier that evening, DeMaria had mentioned that after they crossed the river, a Canadian artillery shell had fallen short and blown up the bridge that Company I would use. The artillery shell blocked their escape and cut off the following companies. The Americans stacked their weapons, but DeMaria claimed that the Germans hid their rifles in the litters used to bear their wounded away. "We were caught with our pants down," DeMaria said. The Germans turned their rifles on the disarmed Americans and took them prisoner.

DeMaria would later tell the most amazing story. Right after the Germans turned their rifles on the GIs:

"There was a Jewish kid from New York in the platoon. We had heard what the Germans did to Jewish soldiers. I told the Jewish kid to get rid of his dog tags with the 'H' for Hebrew and tell them he was protestant. The kid had a Jewish sounding name (Benjamin?). I met up with the kid after the war and he made it through ok."

I remember my dad telling me that he had gotten rid of his dog tags. Incredibly, he ended up in an officer's camp! Without dog tags, the Germans had to guess his rank and assumed he was an officer! The official list of POWs from the Company I Lucherberg engagement shows only one officer. The roster of prisoners at officer's camp where Ben was taken lists only Lt. Varela and Ben. No records of the other POWs could be found (except for DeMaria).

Pvt. Robert H. Hornridge	SSgt. Georg D. Luigard	SSgt. Paul C. Artman
Pfc. Clarence R. Jones	SSgt. Frank Maulden	Pfc. William E. Burris
Pfc. Nathan I King	Pfc. Maurice Sabot	Pfc. Paul Cicio
Pfc. Benjamin Lewis	Pfc. Edgar Turton	SSgt. Elroy A. DeMaria
Pvt. John M. Loftus	2nd Lt. Edwin Varela	Pvt. Alfred L. Barnhouse

Chapter 17

Sadie

SADIE HAD ALREADY GONE THROUGH THE PROCESS of writing letters to a son who was no longer receiving them. I have the letters that were sent back once Charlie was declared MIA. The same happened with Sadie's letters to Ben. The first was sent November 28.

> *"Darling Ben, (Love from everyone)*
> *Today Tuesday November 28 and I'm so sorry that I have not written to you for a few days-the reason: I was so worried about you that I couldn't write. The last letter that I had from you was dated October 20 from Belgium.*

I wrote you (that) another mother heard from her boy in your division on November 8-that letter was written October 20 from Holland and when I didn't hear from you I was so heartbroken. I didn't get the mail yet but darling Edith arranged with her mother to call me as soon as she gets mail for they get mail at 9 AM. Well her mother called me a little while ago that she got a letter dated November 8 but held up for the NY postmark is November 20. She said that you are in Germany. When I get your letter I'll know more and I'll write again this afternoon. I'll send an airmail to you and a V-mail both this afternoon. I'm mailing this right now before the mailman comes. Do be cautious dear and oh how I pray for you-trust no foreigners. Darling may this bloody mess be over and you come home safe and sound to Edith and your loving family.
A world of love. Mom"

Edith received a letter from Ben on December 1, and that same day, Sadie sent him a letter. It was two days before the capture.

"Darling Ben, Today, Friday December 1, a new month. I wish I knew this moment that you are well- there is so much going on in the Western Front that I can't help but worry and your division is mentioned so often in the news. We are all well- in fact everybody here is too well- considering what you boys are going through. No one here is suffering at all. The people's worry is shortages in their likes and conveniences. Some don't feel the war at all. Be cautious darling. Your welfare means so much to my welfare and if you are concerned for me more than

yourself then dear be extra careful and don't do the suicidal acts. Enough danger where you are and in what you are doing. A world of love and may God watch over you and keep you safe from harm. Love from all the family and Dad and Perle and Edith and Mom."

In her letter dated December 6, Sadie updated the situations of various relatives stationed in England, France, and Germany, clearly distraught.

"Why don't those damn Nazis surrender now, it is so obvious that nothing they do now can give them any hope of winning this war. I'm only worried about our fine American boys who are sacrificing life and limb for despite the fact that the casualties are high among the Germans, we are paying a high price too."

Sadie's next letter tries to circumvent the censors to discover Ben's location because for some reason she thought her son was in the 9th Army and had been following their challenges, both in combat and poor weather. So she asked Ben to answer with just a "yes" written to confirm that he was with the 9th. It never came, but he was in fact in the 1st Army.

The returned letter of December 8 indicated that Sadie had received several letters from Ben from late November – the last batch until she would learn his whereabouts as a POW.

"Do be cautious darling. Watch out for the treachery- the Germans mine their dead and put up fake surrender

white flags. Don't trust any of them. Please be extra careful. Think of me at all times and you'll do the right thing, for I want you not to expose yourself to more danger than you are already facing. All my love, Mom."

Sadie started to become frantic as friends, relatives, and even former bosses asked about Ben, and she followed reports of action closely. "I just heard news - your division was mentioned at Duran the 1st Army and 9th Army the 104th together with the 9th infantry division."

As the war intensified, Sadie and Edith drew closer, although that wouldn't last.

"Today Friday December 15- Edith is coming over this afternoon after school. I am mailing a package today, a large package of cookies and candies. Edith had a small can of peaches that she couldn't get into her package so I'll put her can of peaches in my package and we will both go to P.O. to mail it."

As she worried about Ben, Sadie didn't forget her other MIA son. On December 16:

"A little more promising news about Charlie- last night one of the mothers called me on the phone from Baltimore- she received a letter from her son who is a prisoner in Tokyo. It was a printed letter but signed in his own handwriting. He said that he was fine and they write to him 'not to worry'. I called up the pilot's mother in Baldwin [Lt. Nauman] but she didn't hear anything yet. I

hope to God that that news, as pessimistic as it is, would be welcome nevertheless. So let's keep our fingers crossed that we too hear from Charlie."

Here is the letter that Mrs. Cascio received from her son Paul from a Japanese POW camp. Paul was one of the four crew-members who survived the crash on June 1, 1943 that carried Charlie as navigator. She contacted all of the families from Charlie's plane.

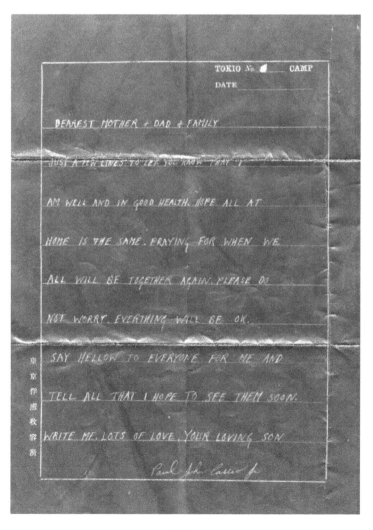

By mid-December, Sadie and the rest of the world were hearing about the Battle of the Bulge, the huge and deadly German counter-offensive not far from Ben[99]. On December 16:

"I feel depressed today because the news is very unfavorable from your region. Since Saturday, December 16, we are hearing how the Germans started a fierce counter-attack against the 1ˢᵗ and 9ᵗʰ Armies, driving you boys from Durian (actually Duren) back to Belgium and Luxembourg. It seems strange that I should write you this when you are actually in it but I wanted you to know that we get the bad news with the good. I also heard that the 104ᵗʰ division was at Durian(sic), so naturally my worries are concerning you."

Just one more letter would come back to Sadie:

"Today is Thursday, December 21–4 days to Christmas and oh what a Christmas for you boys of the 1ˢᵗ Army. I pray to God that he protects you from harm and I am terribly depressed on that account for the news is very unfavorable and the situation grave. We will win the war but it will take so much longer and this counterattack must have been very costly in the lives of our young innocent boys."

During the Battle of the Bulge, the Germans dressed as US soldiers to infiltrate the American lines. "Do be extra cautious darling-they are very treacherous from what I hear. They dress in US uniforms and ride in captured US jeeps and trick our boys close enough to machine gun them. Be on the alert when in doubt trust no friendly foreigners," Sadie wrote.

On December 22, the dreaded telegram arrived. The news devastated Sadie, so she did what she did best. She'd already written to Mrs. Roosevelt to get Ben out of combat. Now she contacted United States Senator Robert Wagner of New York, who forwarded Sadie's request to remove Ben from combat to Colonel W. O. Rawls of the army general staff corps. Colonel Rawls didn't offer any help either:

"It is with the deepest regret that I am obliged to tell you that information has been received at the War Department stating that Private Lewis is missing in action in Germany since 3 December 1944. This report was transmitted to Mr. Hyman Lewis, the soldier's father, on 22 December 1944. No late report concerning the soldier has so far reached the War Department. The sacrifice which Mr. and Mrs. Lewis have been called upon to make is extreme and it is my sincere hope that encouraging news concerning both their sons may soon be received. You may assure them that they will be notified immediately upon the receipt of a report in the War Department."

Then Sadie wrote to General Allen, who replied in what seems a genuine and heartfelt response.

General Allen wasn't just passing the buck when he mentioned having his division's chaplain look into Ben's fate. On January 16, 1945, more than two months since Sadie had heard a single positive word about her son, an encouraging letter arrived from the chaplain, Gerald A. Quinn. Ben and his comrades had been captured while attacking "a hill," and they believed he'd been taken prisoner "unharmed." And then the most concrete news of all:

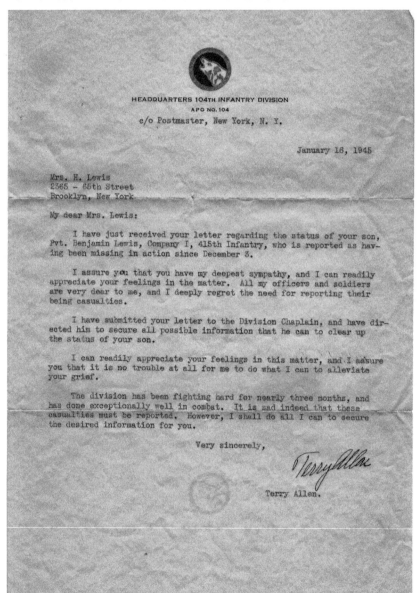

HEADQUARTERS 104TH INFANTRY DIVISION
APO NO. 104
c/o Postmaster, New York, N. Y.

January 16, 1945

Mrs. H. Lewis
2365 – 65th Street
Brooklyn, New York

My dear Mrs. Lewis:

I have just received your letter regarding the status of your son, Pvt. Benjamin Lewis, Company I, 415th Infantry, who is reported as having been missing in action since December 3.

I assure you that you have my deepest sympathy, and I can readily appreciate your feelings in the matter. All my officers and soldiers are very dear to me, and I deeply regret the need for reporting their being casualties.

I have submitted your letter to the Division Chaplain, and have directed him to secure all possible information that he can to clear up the status of your son.

I can readily appreciate your feelings in this matter, and I assure you that it is no trouble at all for me to do what I can to alleviate your grief.

The division has been fighting hard for nearly three months, and has done exceptionally well in combat. It is sad indeed that these casualties must be reported. However, I shall do all I can to secure the desired information for you.

Very sincerely,

Terry Allen.

"A few days ago the Germans announced over their propaganda station a list of names of prisoners. Among them was a Benjamin Lewis, 12220197."

If there was one person in the entire world whom Sadie did not want to hear from, it was Major General James Ulio. He was the adjutant general of the army who had informed her, back in March and June 1943, that Charlie had been wounded, and in a second message, missing in action. But on February 26, Sadie heard officially from General Ulio via Western Union:

"Report just received through the International Red Cross States that your son private first class Benjamin Lewis is a prisoner of war of the German government. Letter of information follows from provost marshal general. Ulio the Adjutant General."

Sadie's neighbor offered support:

"Dear Lewises:
We are overjoyed at the good news you have received
about Ben. The word passed around like fire on East
Fourth Street. All your old neighbors walked around with
smiles on their faces as soon as they were apprised of the
news.
We think of you often and hope you will receive further
good news.
Sincerely,
Rose and Arthur Price and Edythe Ottilie"

Of course Ben wasn't safe, but he was alive.

Perhaps Sadie was thinking ahead. What, if anything, would the government do about war crimes, she wrote to the judge advocate's office. It's not clear what she meant by war crimes, which doesn't apply to being a POW who wasn't tortured or executed, as he would likely have been in the Pacific. Perhaps she was referring to the Japanese. But she got a response:

HQ Army Service Forces, Office of the Judge Advocate General, Washington, DC

14 April 1945
Dear Mrs. Lewis:
I wish to acknowledge receipt of your letter of April 2,
1945, directed to this office, regarding publicity on the
subject of war criminals. With one of your sons a

prisoner in the hands of the Germans and the other listed as missing in action in the South Pacific, I can well understand your deep personal concern in this matter.

I can only point out, however, that the emphasis placed by press and radio upon apprehension of war criminals, actuated no doubt by the feeling that the perpetrators of atrocities against our service men should be warned that they shall not go unpunished, is a responsibility of both the press and radio not subject to government control.

Such few official utterances as have been made in the matter, it is believed, will prove a deterrent rather than an encouragement to reprisals on the part of our enemies.

With genuine appreciation of your views on this subject, I am Sincerely yours, Melvin Purvis, Colonel, JAGD, Acting Director, War Crimes Office

Chapter 18

POW!

BEN WAS HELD FOR A TIME IN OFLAG 64, a prison camp for officers, in Schubin, Poland. We don't know how he got there, but his name is on a list of internees at the camp and Sadie received two postcards from Ben from there. Here's the first "Postkarte," dated January 16, 1945:

Oflag was short for Offizierlager (Officer's camp), a designation that was critical, and Kriegsgefangenen is loosely translated as POW so the GIs called themselves "Kriegies," a bastardization of that German word. Both the Germans and Americans censored these brief missives, but at least Sadie knew her son was alive. How did the private first class (PFC) end up in an officer's camp? It likely that there wasn't insignia on any of the prisoners, and if asked his "name, rank and serial number" Ben would likely have answered truthfully. At the time of evacuation on January 21, Oflag 64 housed 1459 officers and only 136 enlisted men. And it's unlikely that Ben was "impersonating an officer," which would be a crime and not appreciated by his fellow actual officers.

So what happened between Ben's capture on December 3rd and the time that the postcard was sent from Oflag 64? Perhaps the Germans rushed their prisoners away from the front because the Battle of the Bulge was looming. Or they could have killed their prisoners, which happened during the impending battle and frequently to Russian POWs. After the war, Sadie received a document that listed the camps that Ben was probably in. Stalag XIIa in Limburg, Germany, might have been the stop before Oflag 64. So somehow Ben went southwest for a time to Limburg and then probably traveled by train to Poland. Its 435 miles from Lucherberg, Germany, where Ben was captured, to Schubin, Poland.

Excellent first person accounts reveal what life was like for some of the Americans held in Oflag 64[100-11]. Unfortunately Mr. DeMaria, the sergeant captured with my dad who advised him to shed his dog tags, did not give any details about his POW experiences in the weeks after capture. The various accounts from other prisoners captured in and around Lucherberg at or before December 3 all describe a similar experience. The prisoners were marched or trucked away from the front, interrogated for days or weeks, then most likely put on the train to Schubin and Oflag 64.

Ben was awarded a Purple Heart. I have an official letter for "wounds received December 23, 1944" – he was injured 20 days after capture. I'm pretty sure he wasn't shot, but he received a monthly disability check for the rest of his life. So what happened and where did it happen? I don't think he was wounded in the POW camp, but he might have been hurt during the journey to Oflag 64. The experiences of another GI may shed some light on how Ben could have been injured.

Robert Corbin[103] was captured near Aachen on November 26, not far from where Ben had been captured. Corbin, like Ben, wore no insignia. Corbin's captors interrogated him for four days. He then "hitchhiked" 30 miles to Dusseldorf, jumping on any transport he and his guards could find. Upon arrival in Dusseldorf, they just missed a bombing from the US Eighth Air Force. Corbin was placed on a train headed north for Stalag XI B in Fallingbostel, near Hanover. Each train car held 50 men, ten more than the capacity. The two-day trip took four days, with only bread and horse meat to sustain the men. Corbin stayed in Stalag XI B until December 19, when he boarded yet another train, bound for Oflag 64.

Reports from another GI, Jay Drake[105], suggest that Ben was wounded on December 23, en-route to Oflag 64. Also captured near the Siegfried line, Drake mentioned an Allied plane attack as the German boxcar he was in raced its way to Oflag 64, where he arrived on the 24th.

The experience of yet another captured GI adds to the picture of what Ben may have experienced. Captain James Watts[109] was captured near Metz around November 21, 1944, after being stranded in a train yard for days without food and water. Three days later, in Limburg, Watts finally got fed some bread and butter. Limburg is the first camp I believe Ben was briefly held. While at Limburg Watts was de-loused and interrogated. After being ill for a couple of days, on November 29 he was moved to a castle in Dietz, again interrogated and kept in solitary confinement, albeit with better food. By December 2, Watts was back in Limburg and he then spent several days on passenger trains. In one town, loosely guarded and wearing a coat resembling a German Army field coat, he got on a soup line intended for German soldiers, fooling his guards until he went for seconds! Watts was placed on yet another train, where he sat for 52 hours before being moved to Frankfurt am Main. An Allied air attack on a nearby factory just missed his train. After leaving Frankfurt am Main by train on December 12, food ran out on the 15th. Watts finally arrived in Frankfurt am Oder on December 16. After two more days over flat terrain in intense cold, Watts arrived at Oflag 64.

Chapter 19

OFLAG 64[112]

CONDITIONS IN OFLAG 64 weren't too bad if German reports were to be believed. Living quarters were clean. Each prisoner received two blankets and a mattress stuffed with wood shavings. The washroom had 48 faucets, the kitchen a large stove. Lunch included 1/6 loaf of bread and supper a boiled potato with spam or corned beef (from the Red Cross parcels). Prisoners watched films, put on shows, and formed an orchestra. They played sports and produced a newspaper.

The GI point of view was not so glowing. The Germans stole from the Red Cross parcels, running water stopped, and stove fuel supplies ran out. The mail didn't come and the prisoners were always hungry. Was this a Rashomon situation? Which view was true? The consensus seems to have been that the prisoners were indeed cold and hungry, but no more so than local civilians and even the guards. In the winter of 1945 in Poland, the Germans were in retreat and everyone was suffering. The weekly Red Cross parcels seemed to have sustained the men, even with the thefts.

Content of Red Cross Parcels([110,113]):

1 pound powdered milk	1 pound box prunes or raisins	1 pound can oleo margarine	1 can Spam	1 can tuna or salmon
1 can C rations	1 can jam	½ pound cheese	1 pound sugar	1 1/2 oz. coffee
1 small paté (chicken or liver)	1 box biscuits	2 D-bars or cocoa	12 vitamin pills	

Oflag 64[114] was located in the town of Shubin, and it was once a reform school. It had a large, concrete four-story building called "The White House," seven temporary brick barracks, and a smaller building that served as a hospital and chapel. A separate building held latrines. A double barbed wire fence surrounded the camp, ringed by ten-foot high guard towers bearing search lights and swivel-mounted rifles. While Americans essentially ran all operations inside the fence line, POWs would be shot without warning if they crossed the fence. Each day the prisoners participated in "appels," or formations, so the Germans could count them and make announcements. The American officers punished lateness to an appel, typically with prolonged standing at attention in the assembly area.

The senior American officer (SAO), Colonel Paul R. Goode, stayed with the POWs throughout their long and difficult journey. Colonel Goode didn't encourage escape attempts, but he didn't prevent them either. His thinking was that the Russians were getting close and liberation was only weeks away. Their information came from a secret radio. A number of half-finished escape tunnels were discovered when the camp was evacuated on January 21, 1945.

The German commander was the "portly and officious" Oberst (Colonel) Fritz Schneider, according to the prisoners, and the Viennese executive officer, Hauptman Menner, was "kind and apologetic."

The men spoke of boredom, hunger, and cold. Colonel Goode insisted on strict army discipline, which contributed to the high morale and health of the men. He made the men walk an hour every day inside the fence line to train for what was likely to be some kind of long march…how right he was!

Clothing

Long underwear top and bottom	2 pair wool pants	1 wool shirt	1 high neck sweater with sleeves	1 sleeveless sweater
1 short wool jacket with high collar	1 field jacket	1 wool knit cap	1 pair leggings	Towel = muffler
1 pair shoes (sometimes boots)	2 pairs of socks = mittens	Sometimes long overcoat		

Chapter 20

The March[100-112,114,115]

IN LATE JANUARY 1945, the prisoners and guards in Oflag 64 could hear the sounds of Russian artillery. Most of the prisoners felt that it was just a matter of time for liberation by their Soviet Allies. The Germans basically waited too long to expeditiously evacuate the prisoners ahead of the Russian advance. It is believed that Himmler had ordered removal of American and British prisoners so they could later become hostages or bargaining chips. What is not in doubt is that no German wanted to be captured by the Russians given the brutal treatment the Russian POWs had received at the hands of the Germans. So on January 20, the prisoners in Oflag 64 were given 24 hours to prepare to march out of the camp toward an unknown fate. Would this march be like the famous Bataan Death March in the Philippines of April 1942[116]?

In 1942, the Japanese completed their conquest of the Philippines with the final surrender of Corregidor, the island fortress at the tip of the Bataan peninsula on April 9. The war crime that marked this time is known even among those with only a cursory knowledge of the events of World War II. The Japanese marched their Filipino and American captives up the Bataan peninsula to POW camps. Prisoners were beaten and denied food, water, and medical assistance. Those who slowed down or stepped out of line were shot or bayoneted. Hundreds died on the march and more succumbed at the POW camps.

Bataan death march, April 1942

Display at Smithsonian Instituation of American History, Washington, DC.

In contrast to the intentional brutality of the Bataan death march, the terrible conditions of the Oflag 64 march which began on January 21, 1945, were mostly due to inclement weather and too little food, inadequate clothing, and no shelter. Prisoners reported that the German guards, who were older than the GIs and in worse physical shape, suffered through identical conditions. Here is the story.

Guards preparing for the long March[117].

On the morning of January 21, 1945, 27 to 30 platoons of 50 men each began marching through the gates of Oflag 64, including 1200 to 1500 officers and 110 to 135 enlisted men, Ben Lewis among them. The exact numbers aren't known. Left behind were 87 prisoners too sick or incapacitated to march, medical personnel to look after them, and some 50 Americans hiding in the aforementioned partially finished escape tunnels. The Germans had searched for the tunnels in vain just before evacuating the camp.

The prisoners constructed knapsacks from bed sheets and extra clothing, and some jury-rigged sleds and wagons to carry their food and clothing. The march has been described in multiple sources and agree with only slight deviations in details. One thing was true for all the POWs: they were hungry and cold throughout the entire ordeal.

(all March Maps[117])

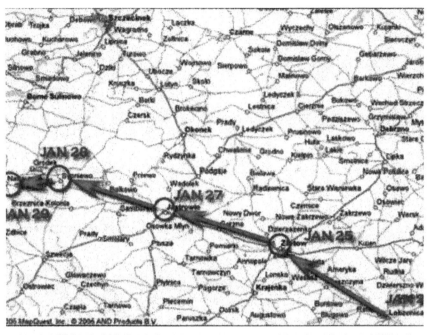

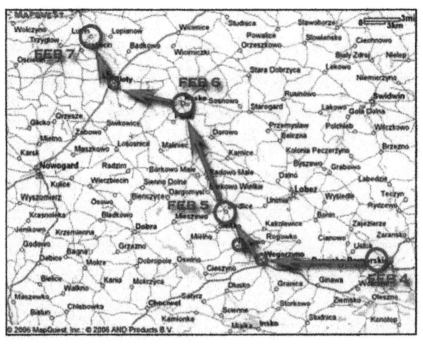

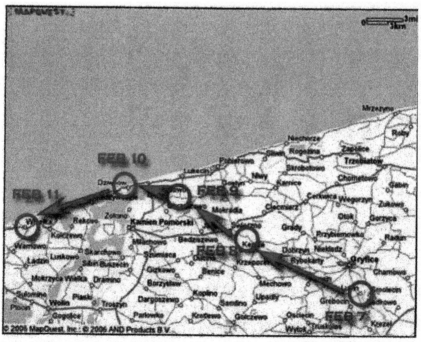

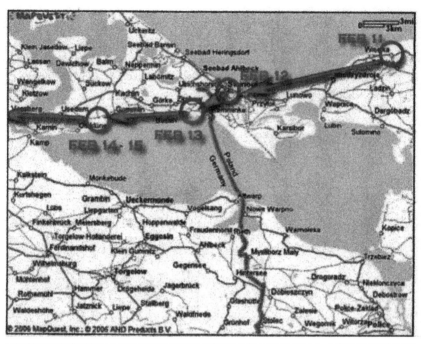

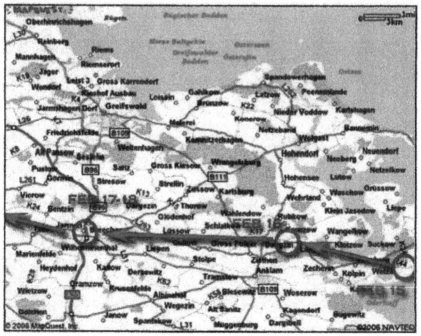

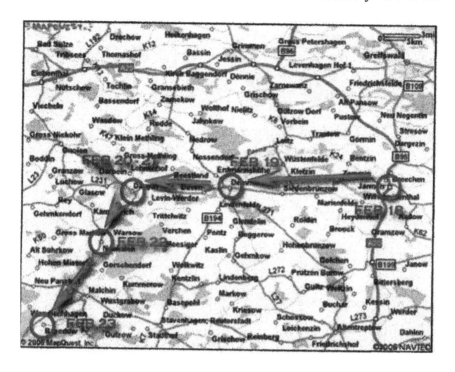

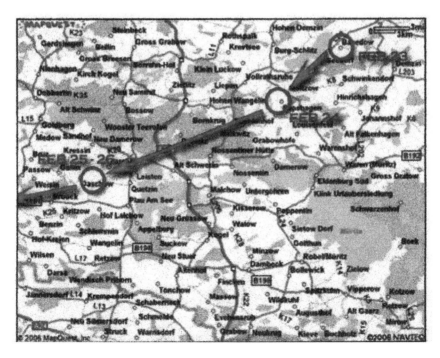

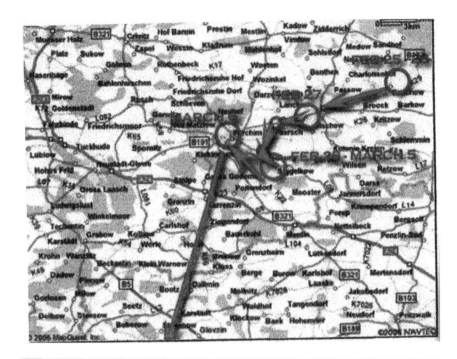

SUNDAY, JANUARY 21, 1945: The temperature was -16°F on the first day of the March. The men walked 21 kilometers to Exin (Kcynia-Polish town names in parentheses), where they slept in a barn owned by a local baron. They carried enough Red Cross food for one week. Many escaped the first day, slipping away from the long line, but Colonel Goode didn't orchestrate any mass exits. He stayed with the column to look after his men. By the time the first POWs entered Exin, the column stretched nearly three miles.

Organization completely broke down when the men stopped. Each man faced a dilemma: should he rush to whatever shelter was available to grab a good spot or queue up for a chance to get some hot food before it ran out? A "good" spot was hard to define. All the way in the back or in the middle would provide the most warmth, but the longer the path to the exit, the more difficult it would be to get out in the pitch black and step over sleeping comrades to relieve oneself. The dysentery due to the contaminated water didn't help matters.

Colonel Goode marched with bagpipes that he did not know how to play, but effectively hid a radio so that the men could keep up with the news. The soldiers learned that on this day Franklin Roosevelt took the oath of office for his fourth term. News of the world they may not have heard was that the Soviet Army had released information on 700,000 Soviet civilians and many others killed by the Germans in Lwow. Evidence indicated violence, torture, and mass killings at death camps. The Germans attempted to cover up their crimes by exhuming and burning their victims[118].

This is a photo of an interfaith pilgrimage march through winter in Poland, taken December 1944. These are not POWs, but it is a scene with which they are likely to have been familiar.
Photo credit: *Skip Schiel.*

MONDAY, JANUARY 22, 1945: The men encountered many refugees on the road, likely German civilians also fleeing the oncoming Russian army. German soldiers were digging in for the coming battle with the Russians.

Many of the POWs had already dropped out of line. That meant one of three things: they'd escaped by ones and twos (about 100) and headed east; they'd fallen behind, too sick to continue (about 25); or they'd been shot by the SS or simply couldn't go on and had probably died of hunger or exposure. The remaining men crossed the Bromberg canal and spent the night in Eichfelds. Here some Polish families provided food.

All of the POWs were combat veterans and now were doing their utmost to survive. Meanwhile, in Washington D.C. Senator James M. Mead (D, NY) told the Senate about an investigation at the Norfolk, VA, Navy Yard. "Men stood and sat around in groups smoking and talking right on the decks of vital fighting ships. There (sic) bosses were nowhere to be seen." Mead added that the men themselves "think" there are too many of them on the job. "They say they are all unable to do an honest day's work[119]."

TUESDAY, JANUARY 23, 1945: The men awoke to a different world: no guards. The Germans had had enough and were trying to make their way home, but unfortunately for them, Latvian SS units returned the guards to the column. Hiding in a barn as an attempt to escape was dangerous for the POWs because the SS would poke at the haylofts with pitchforks or shoot into them. The SS confiscated Oberst Schneider's car as punishment for running away. After that, all the Germans had to walk too.

The world was slow to learn about the brutal conditions of POWs, especially those held by the Japanese. A Vatican representative in

Tokyo visited Camp Nagoya and he reported that thousands of American, Canadian and British prisoners were in "excellent health and spirits[120]."

WEDNEDAY, JANUARY 24, 1945: The march left Charlottenberg in bitter cold and proceeded nine kilometers to Lessens. Poles offered the POWs bread, butter, and cheese even though SS guards threatened to shoot any civilian who aided the Americans. The frigid temperature continued. Curious to me was that the POWs rarely had gloves or mittens, so they wore socks on their hands for warmth. I became a long distance runner in high school and continue to this day. In the winter I've always worn socks on my hands, despite being teased. But it makes perfect sense – the socks hold the fingers together for extra warmth and are easy enough to stow in a pocket if things warm up. Did I learn this trick from my dad?

Food was quite variable on the march. A GI might get oatmeal, or several men would share a loaf of bread. Or he'd get nothing. Occasionally they received margarine or cheese. On this day the POWs had pea soup.

The Russians crossed the Oder River, meaning that the Russians were hot on the tail of their mortal enemy the Germans. Some American POWs were luckier than others. According to a report in the *Brooklyn Eagle*, two "Boro" soldiers were among 15 sick or wounded POWs repatriated by the Germans through Switzerland. Millions of books, games, musical instruments, and sports articles that War Prisoners Aid of the YMCA sent to German POWs, cheered the captive men[121]. Oflag 64 had a jazz band and an orchestra using YMCA instruments.

THURSDAY, JANUARY 25, 1945: On this day, three years before my father would marry Edith, the POWs left Lessens and reached Flatow after a 23 kilometer march. They heard Russian artillery and met more Latvian SS guards. That evening the men again slept in a barn. They tried to help a wounded Russian soldier, but the guards wouldn't let him into the barn. The next morning the Russian was found frozen to death.

Racism directed towards Japanese–Americans was common in the US. In Hollywood, California, an American Legion post of 200 members supported the membership application of an honorably discharged Japanese–American. Dick Horton, district commander, was accused of opposing Harley M. Oka's application specifically and Japanese in general. Japanese–Americans were sent to live in internment camps, yet their eligible sons fought bravely in the US infantry in Europe[122].

FRIDAY, JANUARY 26, 1945: Today was a rest day. Some 87 officers and 4 enlisted men, all too disabled to continue, were put on trains. Everyone else continued on foot. The POWs were given their first bread ration in five days.

Sadly, racism against African Americans was common as well. The United Metals Refining Company of Cartaret, New Jersey, proposed to bring 500 Jamaican "Negroes" to work in the plant and house them in a former Coast Guard barracks. Mayor Leon Schindler reported that a meeting of 50 residents of Clark Township voted unanimously to oppose letting the Jamaicans live in their community[123].

SATURDAY, JANUARY 27, 1945: The men walked 18 kilometers through heavy snow to Jastrow (Jastrowie), where they passed British, French, and Russian POWs, some who had been in captivity since 1939. POWs had their coldest day yet. The Germans moved 120 more POWs, too weak to continue, to Stalag IIIA. The Germans also offered commissions in the German Army to any GI willing to fight the Russians.

There was rampant antisemitism in the American and British foreign-service. American representative Herbert C. Pell was fired over a dispute with the US State Department. Pell favored punishment for Nazi Gestapo members for their crimes against Jews inside their own country. US and British Foreign Service experts said such action would set a bad precedent. "The international law experts contend that what a country does to its own people is its own business. I don't think it's the German's own business because I think their crimes against the Jews have been crimes against humanity," Pell said[124].

SUNDAY, JANUARY 28, 1945: The march continued from Jastrow to Zippnow (Sypniewo). The GIs tramped 18 kilometers through difficult weather. Then they slept in a church after some POWs slaughtered a hog.

Many Axis POWs were sent to camps in the US. The treatment of those POWs was generally quite good, especially compared to what American GIs suffered at the hands of their Axis captors. Private Bernard Hadley fought in New Guinea for two years. He had recently been re-assigned to guard Italian prisoners in a POW camp in San Francisco. "Boy those chaps beat any American GI for griping about their services," said Hadley about the Italians[125]."

MONDAY, JANUARY 29, 1945: The march went on in a continuing blizzard 6 kilometers to Offlag IID, a former Polish officer's camp. Here they re-assembled stoves and cooked potatoes. Only 766 POWs were left from the original column of 1500 or so.

While the GIs were trudging through Eastern Europe, the *New York Times* reported that a poll of 500 school superintendents showed 68% opposed lowering the voting age to 18. The consensus: "18 year-olds are incapable of casting an intelligent vote[126]."

TUESDAY, JANUARY 30, 1945: The men marched 15 kilometers to Machlin (Machliny). The column made some wrong turns where snow obscured the road signs. The POWs saw German anti-tank guns anticipating the coming battle with the Russians. Local people opened their homes to the prisoners.

Before the POWs were captive, they had learned about the perils of unprotected sex. Not everyone back home was happy about this. "Catholics Assail Birth Control" read a headline in the *Brooklyn Eagle*. Catholic leaders denouncing birth control as "race suicide" warned that this country might be left without enough manpower for national defense by the end of the century as a result of dissemination of birth control information to servicemen[127].

WEDNESDAY, JANUARY 31, 1945: The men walked the 12 kilometers to Templeburg (Czaplinek) with the temperature finally rising above freezing. The warmth melted snow that permeated boots, soaking the men's feet and making their lives even more miserable. However, on the way, farmers offered food. The men dried their socks and ate bread and potatoes.

Homefront family members of POWs learned that 9000 next-of-kin were to receive maps showing the location of German POW camps. The American Red Cross held question and answer sessions for the relatives[128]. I have no evidence that Sadie ever received this information.

Thursday, February 1, 1945: The POWs walked five kilometers to Heinrichsdorf (Siemczyno), where the Germans fed them a thick barley soup. The men were all asleep by 11:30 and didn't awaken for 24 hours.

Ben's groups of POWs marching through Poland had it bad but their treatment by their German guards cannot compare to the fate of Americans POWs in the Pacific. An American submarine torpedoed a Japanese ship carrying 750 American POWs. There was no effort by the Japanese to mark the ship as one carrying Americans. Two survivors reported that Japanese on other ships shot at the Americans trying to swim to shore. They witnessed a Japanese officer decapitating Americans with a saber while the men were swimming[129].

Friday, February 2, 1945: After eating more bread, the men walked 18 kilometers to Falkenburg (Zlocieniec) and slept at farms around Zulshagen; it rained most of the way. They saw a great deal of military traffic.

There was a real fear that American POWs held by the Japanese in the Philippines would be killed so the Americans liberated the Japanese POW camp, Carbantuan, on Luzon in a daring raid. One POW, Max Greenberg, hadn't seen his parents in 10 years.

For those lucky enough to survive the war, government benefits would ease the soldiers back to civilian life. Thus Auron Rudy became the first Brooklyn veteran to buy a home with the help of a GI Bill of Rights loan[130].

Saturday, February 3, 1945: The men arrived in Zuelshagen (Suliszew) and had a rest day, enjoying bread and potatoes, some milk, and a "decent stew." They traded cigarettes for food with their Latvian SS guards. The GIs witnessed a Russian POW being shot. They also solved a problem. Up until this point, when the GIs reached a town, their source of shelter was up in the air. Now the Germans gave the POWs' second in command, Major Hazlett, permission to bicycle ahead of the main column to procure sleeping arrangements.

As the Russians continued their push west, the world was slowly learning about the Holocaust. Germans killed millions in their death camps but also as they occupied towns and villages in Eastern Europe. The Soviets announced the names of 100 Germans accused of war crimes. During the German occupation of Lithuania, the Germans killed 165,000 Russian POWs. They also shot, burned alive, or tortured to death 300,000 civilians. Residents of Kaunas called the German enclave there the "Death Fort," where prisoners were stripped naked and shot down into mass graves. The Russians liberated 1000 emaciated prisoners from the Oswiecim "murder factory." Estimates are that 1.5 million Russians, Poles, Jews, Czechs, French, and Yugoslavs were killed at this camp, better known today as Auschwitz[131,132].

Sunday, February 4, 1945: The POWs walked 17 kilometers to Gienow (Ginawa). They arrived in the late afternoon, but were forbidden to make fires as punishment for someone stealing a chicken.

Sadie went long periods of time without any news about the fate of Charlie or Ben. But others heard. Mrs. Anita Hurt of Queens had received a telegram stating that her son Flight Officer William C. Hurt's plane was "crippled" in a bombing run over Hungary. She later received word that her son's plane was trying to reach Yugoslavia. Then no word. Mrs. Elizabeth Reaney lived across the street from Mrs. Hurt and her son Sergeant John Fitzpatrick was in the same outfit as William. Mrs.

Reaney wrote to her son and he reported that William was just fine, back in action[133]!

MONDAY, FEBRUARY 5, 1945: The men set out early and walked 20 kilometers to Zeitlitz (Wegorzyno), hearing that more men would be sent to trains. Soon, trucks transported 180 men to the Ruhnow train station, where these men with guards were sent on to the final destination, Stargard. The rest dragged on by foot. When walkers stopped for the night, Russian POWs ladled out soup with cabbage, noodles, and meat.

Unbeknownst to the marching POWs, as the Germans were retreating from Poland, they were continuing their crimes against humanity. Germans murdered between 1000-3000 prisoners in the Radogscz compound as they evacuated Lodz. Correspondents found hundreds of burned bodies on the floor of the former textile factory. Only 877 of the pre-war Jewish population of 250,000 survived the German occupation. One of the survivors, Albert Mazur, a Lodz physician, wrote to relatives in Brooklyn. Mazur survived by hiding in evacuated ghetto buildings[134].

TUESDAY FEBRUARY 6, 1945: The men awoke and had oatmeal and the ever-present potatoes for breakfast, and then walked 20 kilometers to a slave labor camp in Regenwalde (Resko). On this day began the practice of the Germans delivering warm "coffee" in a horse drawn wagon carrying an old boiler. The men referred to their noon beverage as "ersatz coffee" because it frequently was made with everything from vegetables to grass. That night the men slept in the barracks of the slave labor camp.

In the Philippines, Manila fell to the Americans[135].

The *Brooklyn Eagle* reported about another Brooklyn hero. Margaret Quent's husband Robert was killed in action in November. Mrs. Quent accepted the Scouting Heroes Award for her late husband. Robert had been a scout master before the war. This was the first time the Scouts gave out this award posthumously[136].

WEDNESDAY, FEBRUARY 7, 1945: Another 20 kilometer trek took the men through Plathe, to Lilbin (Ploty). Deteriorating boots and wet feet were taking their toll.

The fight for freedom abroad continued to bump up against stories of racism at home. Dr. Selig A. Shevin, a staff member at Jackson Park Hospital in Chicago, resigned to protest the hospital's refusal to admit an American-born Japanese patient[137].

Supreme Court Justice Meier Steinbrink of Brooklyn criticized a report submitted by the council on dental education and the American Dental Association limiting admission of students to dental school based on a racial quota. "Coming at a time when America's sons and daughters of every race, religion and national origin are giving their lives in a common cause, the recommendations of the committee constitute a deplorable repudiation for which they are fighting," the justice said[137].

THURSDAY, FEBRUARY 8, 1945: The prisoners went on yet another 20-kilometer march, this time to Stuchow (Stuchowo). The ubiquitous boiled potatoes and some ersatz coffee couldn't replace the calories the POWs were burning. That evening the men ate carrot soup and potatoes and then slept in haylofts. A few lucky prisoners feasted with slave labor families on a dinner of pancakes, syrup, beans, and milk.

On this date, Daniel Harris, the last surviving Civil War veteran from Brooklyn, died at age 98. He was also the last of 8000 Jews who fought for the Union[138].

FRIDAY FEBRUARY 9, 1945: Today it was on through Stresow, arriving in Grosse Justin (Gostyn) after a rainy 14-kilometer march. The POWs were served potatoes and some got milk.

The POWs often wrote that they should have made a break for freedom. However, life on the run was treacherous as well. Sergeant Warren E. Maue and PFC Richard W. Hartman made it safely back to American lines after hiding from the Germans for 23 days. The two men were separated from their unit when they were ordered to "escape individually" during an engagement with the Germans. Both men lost 40-50 pounds. They hid in a hayloft and survived on melted snow, dried corn from a rabbit hutch, potato peelings, rotten plumbs, and plumb wine[139].

SATURDAY, FEBRUARY 10, 1945: The POWs marched to Dievenrow (Dziwnow) along the Baltic Sea, crossing the Oder River. The prisoners passed through the "Goering Home for Children." They slept in the barracks of a Luftwaffe camp that had electric lights, a working stove, and better food. The POWs saw Hitler Youth marching and singing.

A series of surveys by the United Auto Workers vividly illustrated "the rise and fall of women in wartime industry." The surveys explored activities and expectations of women war workers. Layoffs were just beginning; other employment options didn't look good:

72% of the women had no other job

25% were offered jobs that were too physically demanding

14% were working day-shifts but couldn't take late afternoon or midnight shifts.

The surveys also noted the widespread discrimination against Negro women[140].

SUNDAY, FEBRUARY 11, 1945: The men arrived in Neuerdorf (Wiselka) after a 15- kilometer march. That night they endured very crowded sleeping arrangements.

As the Germans retreated, the remaining Jews still faced serious threats. Eliahu Dobkin, head of the immigration department of the Jewish Agency in Palestine, estimated that 1.2 million Jews survived of the six million under German rule. Most were eager to come to Palestine. The surviving Jews faced an uncertain future. "There is open antisemitism and a hostile attitude to the vestiges of the Jewish community that remains in Poland," General Wladyslaw Zavalzyk, deputy commander of the Polish Army said.[141]

Repatriating Jews to their country of origin wouldn't work because the Jews "have no means of existence and no prospects or reintegration in economic life" (in their former countries), said Dobkin, mentioning restrictions on entering Palestine. Before the war, those opposing Jewish settlement claimed there were too many of them and now they were saying too few, he added.

MONDAY, FEBRUARY 12, 1945: Colonel Goode calculated that the men had walked 235 miles in 23 days. Thirty-nine men were too sick and malnourished to continue, but German officer Hauptman Menter resisted letting them stay behind. Finally, four GIs were left in a hospital and the Germans arranged for trucks to carry the packs of the other sick men. The rest of the men walked 20 kilometers to Swinemunde (Swinoujscie), to a German naval base, where the men enjoyed the rare luxury of heated barracks.

On this day the Latvian SS departed because they weren't allowed to enter Germany. The "regular" guards were glad to be rid of the SS and happy to be back in their home country. Marines at the naval base offered the POWs food but the Oflag commander refused their offer.

World War II did help break down some racial barriers. The first all-Negro fighter Squadron (Tuskegee Airmen) was now seeing action in Italy. The airmen returned a $1000 gift from a Detroit union local with the request that it be used to better "interracial goodwill." The money would be used to set up an annual award to a person who promotes social justice[142,143].

TUESDAY, FEBRUARY 13, 1945: The men trudged nine kilometers to Gorz, through a blizzard. Four POWs escaped, possibly with help from the Kriegsmarine. Some POWs thought the escapees had stolen a boat and sailed to Sweden.

Black men could fight for their country yet a fight in Albany, New York, erupted over the proposed Ives-Quinn Bill that would outlaw racial and religious discrimination. Opponents won a demand for a public hearing. CIO State President Louis Hollander said he would mobilize one million union members to support the bill[144].

WEDNESDAY FEBRUARY 14, 1945: The men ate potatoes for breakfast and then marched 14 kilometers in the rain to Stolpe. Passing through Dargen on its cobblestone streets was hard on the men's feet, inspiring POW Victor Kanners to write a memoir of his experience, "Horseshit and Cobblestones."

The Germans selected 100 POWs to board a train to Luckenwalde. Sadly, just as the German retreat from Poland left a trail of death, so did the Japanese retreat from Manila. There were reports from civilians of wholesale slaughter of men, women and children within the Japanese lines[145].

THURSDAY, FEBRUARY 15, 1945: A rest day. The POWs found a German cobbler who repaired their footwear. The upgraded shoes made a big difference. Many of the repaired shoes lasted until the men were on their way home.

Where Sadie failed, the Pappas family succeeded. Sargent Stavros Pappas of Manhattan was on his way home from the Belgian front after a family appeal to President Roosevelt. One of his brothers had been killed and another was MIA[146].

FRIDAY, FEBRUARY 16, 1945: While the 100 selected men stayed behind to await their train, the rest of the men marched 24 kilometers to Anklam. They were led by Lt. Colonel John Waters, General George S. Patton's son-in-law. Colonel Waters' presence would be very important in about six weeks. At the end of the march the men ate cabbage soup, potatoes, and a waferbread called Knackebrod. News from their secret radio claimed that the Russians and the Americans were closing the noose around the Germans...just hold on a little longer.

Major Billy Southworth, Jr., was the first professional baseball player to enlist. He won the Distinguished Flying Cross, completing 25 raids over Europe flying a B-17. Southworth was killed on this day when his B-29 crashed off LaGuardia Field into Flushing Bay[147].

SATURDAY, FEBRUARY 17, 1945: After a 26-kilometer trek to Gutzkow, the men were completely shaved of all body hair to remove lice, while Colonel Goode went ahead and returned with Red Cross parcels. The men stayed at the estate of a "Grafin" (countess) whose husband was a POW of the Americans. The POWs assured the Grafin that her husband was being well-treated.

Racial equality would have a long road to travel. Representative P. Clark Fisher (D, Texas) said that creation of a permanent Fair Employment Practices Commission would "stir up more racial and religious prejudice than this nation had seen in many a moon." The actions of the US House Labor Committee in approving the measure were, "nefarious," he claimed. "We are in the midst of a war and we should be united against the enemy," he added. The bill would give the board the power to decide when a private employer was guilty of racial or religious discrimination in hiring employees. Fisher expected the vast majority of Southern legislators to oppose the bill[148].

SUNDAY, FEBRUARY 18, 1945: The men enjoyed their Red Cross parcels as they rested. Only 490 men were left, Ben among them.

Flying officer J.P. Crisp parachuted from his night bomber and fell through the roof of a Belgian farmhouse. "I had bailed out into the bedroom of the farmer's daughter who screamed at his unexpected entry[149]."

Mrs. Harriet Giebocki was a volunteer Red Cross worker going through telegrams from 33 refugees that listed Brooklyn relatives. These were people that were caught by the Germans while working in Poland and now were being repatriated. One was Mrs. Charlotte Zuber, Mrs. Giebocki's first cousin. Zuber, from Brooklyn, had gone to Sweden and then traveled to Poland and was trapped there when the Germans invaded[149].

MONDAY, FEBRUARY 19, 1945: The men had difficulty covering the 11 kilometers to Tutow because they all had the "runs" from gorging on the Red Cross parcels. When people are starving and then they eat too much, bad things happen to the digestive system.

In 2017 the site of the old Brooklyn Navy Yard is an industrial park and a high-end rental location. On February 19, 1945, the old Brooklyn Navy Yard turned 144. Top brass and politicians attended the celebration at the Yard. The Navy Yard was the largest ship-building facility in the rural and was in serious need of additional workers. The government originally paid $5 for the land in 1801. In 1944, 1,616 vessels were serviced or repaired there. In 1945, 68,000 worked at the Yard, about 6,000 of them women[150].

TUESDAY, FEBRUARY 20, 1945: A 22-kilometer walk through Demmin led to more Red Cross parcels, some American and some Canadian. The moldy biscuits caused some digestive distress but Canadian bacon was most welcome.

Folks back home in New York City were trying to continue "life as normal" despite the war. The so-called, "Cinderella Decree" by War Mobilization Director James F. Byrnes brought many complaints. It ordered all places of entertainment to be closed by midnight. "Why my business doesn't even start at least until 11:00 o'clock at night, 95% of it is done after midnight," complained Mae Flynn, owner of Flynn's Cabaret on Washington Avenue. Miss Flynn had 23 employees including band, waiters, bartenders, and hat-check girls. Many would have to be let go. Joseph Savino, owner of Alp Tavern on 5th Avenue, estimated that his business would be cut in half[151].

WEDNESDAY, FEBRUARY 21, 1945: Another rest day. The POWs were spread out in Demmin, Walkow, and Eugenienburg. The men had soup and traded with locals for additional food. Their pirate radio reported that the Russians had liberated 7000 British, 2000 Serb, and 1000 American POWs. Some in the group must have been regretting their decisions to stay on the march rather than escaping east.

Sadie could not have been too happy to read an article reporting that American POWs in Germany were being marched deeper into the Reich through temperatures 30 degrees below zero without proper clothing, according to Richard F. Allen, vice chairman of the American National Red Cross. "Those of you who have someone in the German prison camps must be ready for some bad news. They are being marched 12 ½ miles a day[152]."

THURSDAY, FEBRUARY 22, 1945: A noon stop for coffee broke up a 16-kilometer walk to Neukalen. Two Red Cross boxes loaded down each man. When the POWs passed by an old Cavalry "Caserne" (barracks), they traded for food with German school boys who were quite fluent in English.

The country Ben and his comrades left behind, was slowly changing. Negroes voting in their primary elections, "is inevitable," said Florida Attorney General J. Thomas Watson to a group of Florida Democratic Party leaders. "It can be done in a way that will reduce the evils. I know I am playing with fire politically," he added. The Negro and white man in American idealism are entitled to, "the same political rights," he said.[153]

FRIDAY, FEBRUARY 23, 1945: February 23 was rainy, with a 19-kilometer hike to Basedow, still fueled by those Red Cross parcels. Meanwhile, the Soviets crossed the Oder River.

Some POWs held by the Germans got home sooner than others. Mrs. Julia Porges of Forest Hills, Queens, learned that the Germans were going to repatriate her son PFC medic Alan A. Porges. Porges was captured December 22 when he was separated from his unit while treating two injured Germans. Porges was one of 27 medical corpsmen Germany released.[154]

SATURDAY, FEBRUARY 24, 1945: The march continued 22 kilometers to Crammar.

Corporal Joseph P. Keys was released from a Japanese POW camp in the Philippines and was looking forward to seeing his "sweetheart" Anne Marie Connelley of Brooklyn. He didn't know that Anne Marie had been married for one year to a sailor. Anne Marie said she had met Keys once or twice and corresponded with him, but his letters stopped. Her husband was home on leave and asked that her married name not be used[155].

SUNDAY, FEBRUARY 25, 1945: The march moved on to Plauerhagon.

Thirteen Brooklyn and Long Island families found out that their relatives were freed from the Santo Tomas prison, where the Japanese had held them since early 1942. Mrs. Gabriel E. Howie's sister-in-law and brother-in-law were in Manila representing the family clothing business when the Japanese took over. Sister-in-law Dorothy had given birth to a baby girl on December 24, 1941 during the Japanese bombing of Manila and had a second baby while in prison in August 1943[156].

MONDAY, FEBRUARY 26, 1945: Rest. Workers the POWs met snuck food to the Americans. The POWs learned that they had three more days of marching and then six days by train, which actually turned out to be three days.

In some ways Ben was lucky to be captured before the Battle of the Bulge where so many Americans were killed. Lieutenant Joseph MacGregor was the first American to land on D-Day and was killed in action January 9, 1945 in Bastogne, Belgium. MacGregor had returned to duty December 31 after being wounded for the second time. He had landed in France on June 5, 1944 before the main body of Americans and had fought for six days behind enemy lines. Before the war, MacGregor had been a teller at New York Bank and Trust[157].

Chapter 21

The March Ends

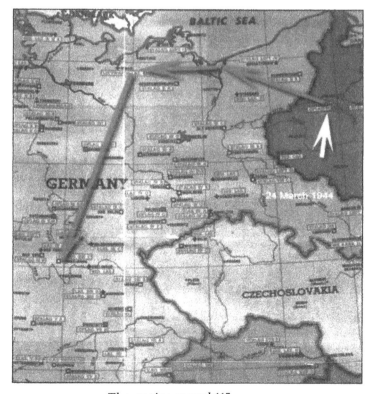

The entire march[117].

By February 27, the men were heading west along the Baltic, through Lubz to Latheran. Partial Red Cross parcels arrived the next day. The men completed their last leg, a 15-kilometer walk to Siggelkow and 7 kilometers to Parchim.

On March 1 the men finally stopped and were issued postcards to send home. Ben wrote his second letter from "his prison camp," likely from Parchim. In his droll way and of course because of censorship Ben wrote:

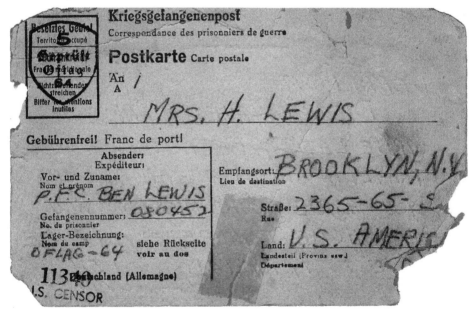

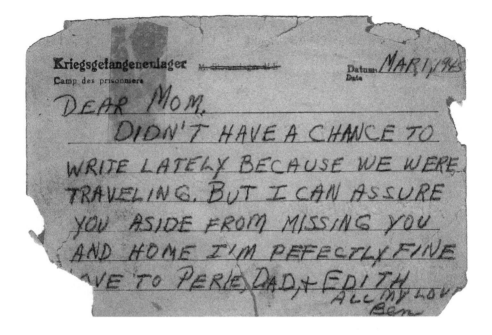

Kriegsgefangenenlager   Datum: MAR 1, 1945
Camp des prisonniers   Data

DEAR MOM,
    DIDN'T HAVE A CHANCE TO
WRITE LATELY BECAUSE WE WERE
TRAVELING. BUT I CAN ASSURE
YOU ASIDE FROM MISSING YOU
AND HOME I'M PEFECTLY FINE
..VE TO PERIE DAD, + EDITH
                      ALL MY LOV..
                          Ben

Ben's "because we were traveling" could have been irony or caution, it's hard to tell. During this time the men saw German jet planes flying overhead – the first jet planes in history. They had a small impact on the war mostly because the engines tended to burn out after a short flight. The famous African American Tuskegee airmen also reported seeing German jet planes. Max Schmelling, the famous boxer who fought Joe Louis, visited the prisoners waiting in Parchim. The postmark of March 1 on Ben's letter from "Oflag 64" confused me for some time because they had left Oflag 64 in January. I later learned that the paper was from his now-abandoned prison camp.

On March 6 the remaining 488 men finally boarded trains marked "US POW" for the three-day trip to Stalag XIII in Hammelburg, the label keeping friendly fire away. This was the prison camp featured in the 1960s TV show Hogan's Heroes[158]. Since January 21 the men had walked 362 miles, in 33 out of 39 days. Forty men were in each car. The German colonel addressed the POWs one last time, saying he hoped they had a speedy return to their loved ones.

At the camp at Hammelburg, Colonel Goode was again the senior American and immediately addressed the poor morale and discipline. The camp was (again) mostly an officer's camp and most of the men had been captured in the Battle of the Bulge. Colonel Goode ordered all 1500 POWs to clean up and prepare for liberation.

In March 1945 Stalag XIII [102,103,159] had 1291 officers and 127 enlisted men, which included the 423 officers and 67 enlisted men from Oflag 64. Approximately 200 men were crowded into each five-room barrack. Each room contained two drop lights of 15 watt bulbs. During extreme cold the men wore all their clothing and huddled around the one stove in each room, allotted 48 coal briquettes for three days. The small fuel ration kept the barrack temperature average about 30 degrees. At the insistence of Colonel Goode, small details were permitted to "scrounge" for pieces of wood to supplement the fuel supply. Washrooms didn't exist and the prisoners had to carry water from the kitchen faucet to a few wash basins in each room. No hot water was available because of the fuel shortage, and the toilet facilities were completely inadequate.

The prisoner's daily menu for the men in Stalag XIII consisted of one-tenth of a loaf of bread, one cup of ersatz coffee, one bowl of barley soup, and one serving of a vegetable. They received a small piece of margarine about three times a week, and an occasional tablespoon of sugar. With this meager diet, by the end of March, many of the officers were dangerously malnourished.

The POW camp also housed many Serbian officers. They saved many American lives with extra food from their own Red Cross packages.

The long march and poor food compromised the health of the prisoners, preventing quick recoveries from such minor ailments as colds, dysentery, trench foot, and influenza. No wonder when later they were briefly liberated by a failed US attack, few had the strength to escape to the American lines.

What happened to the men who didn't arrive at Stalag XIII in Hammelburg? The Russian 61st Army picked up the men left behind in Oflag 64, but they didn't exactly liberate these men, or any other Americans they found. A few GIs even took up arms and fought with the Russians. After captivity and lengthy diplomatic negotiations, most POWs were put on a ship in Odessa and finally made it home to the US. Some of the men who had fallen behind during the long march were killed, died, or were picked up by the SS and sent to either Buchenwald or Dachau concentration camps, where some survived[117].

How did my father, a Jewish GI and POW of the Germans, avoid a concentration camp? Happenstance helped. He'd followed the good advice to pitch his dog tags, and retired Luftwaffe who were not hardcore party members ran some of the camps. So unless SS or Gestapo visited a camp, Jews weren't rounded up for transport. The case of Master Sergeant Roddie Edmonds is particularly moving[160].

Edmonds, not Jewish, was captured during the Battle of the Bulge and sent to Stalag IX. Jewish soldiers captured on the Western Front could be sent to Berga, a slave labor camp where survival rates were low.

One day in January 1945, a month after Edmonds's capture, the Germans ordered all Jewish POWs to report outside their barracks the following morning. Edmonds knew what awaited the Jewish men under his command, so he decided to resist the directive. He ordered all his men — Jews and non-Jews alike — to fall out the following morning. Upon seeing all the soldiers lined up, the camp's commandant, Major Siegmann, approached Edmonds and ordered him to identify the Jewish soldiers.

"We are all Jews here," Edmonds said.

Irate, the commandant jammed his pistol against Edmonds' head and repeated the order. Again, Edmonds refused.

"We are all Jews here. According to the Geneva Convention, we only have to give our name, rank, and serial number. If you shoot me, you will have to shoot all of us, and after the war you will be tried for war crimes."

*Master Sergeant Roddie Edmonds, from Chris Edmonds and the
Times of Israel[160].*

The Jewish Foundation for the Righteous posthumously
honored Edmonds with its "Yehi Or" (Let There Be Light) Award.

Chapter 22

The Raid

REMEMBER THE BOOK that my father gave my brother and me about a raid on a POW camp in Germany? That was his camp, and here's what happened.

George S. Patton was a controversial and famous general[161]. By the time Ben was in Stalag XIII, Patton was in charge of the US 3rd Army and by March 1945 he had led his armored divisions across Europe and into Germany. Books and films, notably one starring George C. Scott[162], have captured the general very well. One incident was particularly telling. It was important to Patton's gigantic ego that his army cross the Rhine River into Germany before his British counterpart and bitter rival, Bernard Montgomery, did so. Patton drove to the front line and began to cross the just-erected pontoon bridge. Then he stopped in the middle and urinated into the river[163].

On a more relevant and serious note, General Patton's son-in-law, Major John Waters, had been captured in the North Africa campaign. Major Waters, as mentioned earlier, was a fellow prisoner with Ben in Oflag 64 and with Ben completed the long march to Stalag XIII. While not certain, most accounts agree that Patton knew his son-in-law was a prisoner in Stalag XIII and ordered a raid to rescue him.

In the fictional movie "Saving Private Ryan[47]," American soldiers have the single mission to find and remove from harm's way Private Ryan because his brothers had been killed in action. Was it ethical to risk the lives of many GIs to save one man? In the true story of the raid on Stalag XIII, Patton ordered a small task force to liberate his son-in-law even without infantry or air cover and 60 miles behind enemy lines. Patton knowingly sent men to die in order rescue Major Waters.

Captain Abe Baum led the task force[164] of 294 men and 53 vehicles, including Sherman tanks, light tanks, and troop carrier half-tracks. Baum's group encountered heavy fighting while crossing the German lines, had smooth sailing for a time, and then became embroiled in a major battle only a few miles from Stalag XIII. Fortunately for Ben and his fellow POWs, the sudden arrival of Baum's task force surprised the Germans in the Hammelburg area, but the enemy quickly recovered and counter-attacked.

Two key events happened that day, March 27: the POWs heard the gun battle between Baum's task force and the Germans outside the gates, and rumors abounded of evacuating camp. General Gunther von Goeckel, a veteran of World War I who ran Stalag XIII, ordered the Americans into bomb shelters, warning Colonel Goode that his soldiers would shoot into the camp if the prisoners became disorderly.

General von Goeckel received orders to defend the Stalag with camp guards, most of whom were old men and World War I veterans like him. And so the last bit of combat of the task force was against the elderly camp guards. Yet the older men put up quite a strong defense, inflicting many casualties upon the Americans, damaging vehicles and destroying all of Baum's extra fuel. Because of the heavy fighting and the shooting into the Serb compound in the camp, the Germans and POWS approached the attacking Americans with a white flag. Although it isn't clear whether von Goeckel surrendered to Goode, the German flag came down as a makeshift American flag went up.

The five-man white flag truce group included American second-in-command John Waters (yes, Patton's son-in-law) and the German second-in-command Hauptman Fuchs. As the truce committee exited the main gate carrying the white flag, a German soldier rose up and shot Major Waters, severely wounding him. Fuchs immediately disarmed the shooter. The truce committee then abandoned their mission so they could get Waters to the Serbian hospital as fast as possible. And so the very person Baum had come to liberate from the camp was now seriously wounded and not able to be liberated. Ironically, Fuchs died a few days later during an American bombing raid.

American tank breaking through the fence of Stalag XIII[165].

Chapter 23

Liberation and the Journey Home

SHORTLY AFTER THE FAILED PEACE INITIATIVE, Baum's men finally subdued the German defenders and his tanks entered the camp, taking down the fencing. The American POWs must have been ecstatic, assuming their day of liberation had come, but some of them may have remembered the time in January when the men in Oflag 64 had also thought freedom was near in the echoes of the distant gunfire of the Soviet army. Now, POWs raided the food warehouse and a few made a dash for freedom. Baum's men lingered at the camp for at least two hours, tending to the wounded, trying to locate Waters, and trying to figure out what to do with all the prisoners.

Ben and his fellow POWs were in no shape to fight their way back 60 miles to the American lines. They were malnourished if not starving, sick or injured, and insufficiently clothed. Yet Colonel Goode gave them three choices[112,115].

Option 1: try to make their way to safety alone.
Option 2: join Baum's task force headed to the American lines.
Option 3: stay put.

About 500 of the POWs attempted to leave the camp on their own, but only 30 made it back safely to American lines. At first option 2 made sense as a way to try to get to the American lines with the tanks of Baum's task force. But it became quickly obvious that Baum didn't have the room nor the supplies to take even few, let alone hundreds of prisoners back with him. So while several hundred POWs started leaving with Baum, including Colonel Goode, after only a few minutes Goode announced he was going back to the camp and most of the prisoners followed him, choosing option 3. They stayed put.

The trek back to the American lines for Baum, his remaining men, and the dozen POWs still with him was short-lived. While Baum and his force had been fighting their way into the camp and then spending some time there, the Germans set a deadly trap. Shortly after Goode and his group left, German fire destroyed Baum's task force, hitting every vehicle. "Every man for himself!" Baum bellowed. Only one member of Baum's unit made it back to friendly lines; everyone else was killed or captured. Baum was wounded and ended up at the Serbian hospital.

But that wasn't all. While the bedraggled and dispirited prisoners were making their way back to the camp, the German guards were rounding everyone up for the planned evacuation that had been rumored just before the raid. Ben and his mates found themselves on the road again, this time heading to Stalag 7a in Moosberg, where the Germans assembled some 15,000 American POWs for final liberation. Ben's official service record lists the POW camps he was in and Moosberg is the last stop before his liberation on May 7. Paul Goode was listed as the last senior American POW at Stalag 7a, and it's likely that Ben was part of his group. I do not know the path Ben took from Hammelburg to Moosburg. I have no record of what happened to Ben from March 28, 1945 to late April 1945 when he arrived in Stalag 7a. Clarence R. Meltesen[115] describes five or six paths the POWs followed after the failed raid leading to their liberation. We can eliminate the paths that did NOT lead to Moosburg. Ben had been with Colonel Goode since his time in Oflag 64, so it is possible that he stayed with Goode's group on their way to Mossburg. If so, Ben left with Colonel Goode by train to Nurnberg (better known as Nuremberg).

The group that went by train with Colonel Goode included men too weak or injured to march. The train ride took three days. Was Ben injured? My brother believed that my father was wounded twice. We share a vague memory of a story in which my father was hurt in the raid on Hammelburg. In fact, we have two Purple Hearts but only one official letter acknowledging a war wound worthy of a Purple Heart from December 23, 1944. But a newsletter from American Legion Post 1300 dated June 1946 had a memorial to Charles H. Lewis that mentioned that his brother Benjamin was "twice wounded."

Or, maybe Ben marched to Moosburg. Allied planes constantly swooped down and fired on the marching POWs, so the men rigged bedsheets to form the letters "USPW" to wave off attacking friendly planes. At least it was warmer than the march from Oflag 64 to Hammelburg.

On April 29, American forces liberated Stalag 7a[166] and Ben was a POW no more. As usual, nothing went smoothly. A brief battle ensued when the Germans rejected an attempt to declare the area around the camp a neutral zone. Now Germans were fighting Germans, some wanting to surrender and others wanting to fight to the last man.

The failed raid at Hammelburg remained secret well into the 1960s. *The New York Times*[167] mentioned a German radio broadcast announcing that American tanks (Baum's task force) were east of Aschaffenburg (near Hammelburg). A day later, the *Times* reported that an American armored column had reached Hammelburg. The American authorities didn't comment on this report or the raid, and after that it wasn't mentioned again.

Ben's story blurs after liberation, with no information on how he got home. Many former POWs ended up in camp Lucky Strike in France[168], and Ben did return home by ship sometime in June 1945, so maybe he was there. He was home in time to attend Edith's high school graduation. After being reunited with his parents, his sister, and Edith, Ben was sent to Lake Placid for "classes," but really to recover from his ordeal. He was briefly assigned to Camp Lee in Virginia before final discharge, on

November 21, 1945. He was 5'10", 150 pounds. Was Ben lucky? A letter he received once home reveals how much worse it could have been:

July 2, 1945
Dear Benjamin,

I note in this morning's paper that you have been fortunate enough to be liberated from a German prison and I certainly want to take this opportunity in wishing you the very best of luck.

In my anxiety to get some information about my son, who has been missing in action since the Belgium Bulge in December, I am reaching out to try to pick up whatever threads of information I can get.

My son was with the 106th Infantry Outfit in the 424th Regiment and during the Belgium Bulge this outfit had about 7,000 men missing in action.

The thought occurred to me that possibly you might have been with the 106th and if so, you might have some information of the 424th Regiment in Company "K." My son's name is Sergeant Morton Kinberg and he was a platoon commander.

If by chance you may happen to know anything about this particular outfit and whether they were taken prisoners, it would give us a thread of hope and, to say the least, a sense of joy.

I am enclosing herewith a self-addressed stamped envelope awaiting a reply, also a photograph of my son. Please return this photograph after it has served your purpose.
Sincerely,
A. Kinberg,
c/o H.L. Green Company, Inc., 902 Broadway, NY

Ben's life after the army went well. He married Edith in Brooklyn on January 25, 1948. He finished school on the GI bill at City College. His previous engineering courses had interested him in pursuing a technical degree, but none of the big companies would hire a Jew. So Ben earned an accounting degree and eventually worked for the IRS. In 1960, he started Brooklyn Law School at night while working days at the IRS. He graduated second in his class in 1964 and opened his own firm with colleagues from the IRS.

Ben and Edith had two sons. Charles H. Lewis, named for Ben's brother was born December 7, 1950, nine years to the day after the attack on Pearl Harbor. I was born March 29, 1954. Ben died from lung cancer on January 31, 1993. The Germans couldn't kill him, but the cigarettes did.

Chapter 24

The Fate of Charlie and His Crew

ON SATURDAY, OCTOBER 19, 1946, Jewish war veterans gathered at Synagogue Ahavath Achim in Brooklyn. There the veterans officially named their Post 520 of the Jewish War Veterans, the Lt. Charles H. Lewis J.W.V. Post, in honor of the sacrifice Lieutenant Lewis gave to his country. Benjamin Lewis was elected as the post's first commander. Ben Lewis also gave the main speech to the assembled group.

In 1943, Sadie and Hyman received a letter from General Kenney. Still no word about Charlie's fate, but one of his crew was "safe" as a prisoner of the Japanese. Charlie had been promoted to first Lieutenant and awarded the Silver Star for his actions over the

Bismarck Sea on March 2, 1943. Hyman accepted the medal on December 6, 1943, at Mitchel Field on Long Island. The letter also credited Charlie with 13 combat missions as of May 20, 1943, fewer than the number in Charlie's flight records, but perhaps not all of them were combat per se. On February 26, 1946, the family received official word from General Carl Spaatz that Charlie had indeed been killed in combat.

LT. CHARLES H. LEWIS POST

No. 520

Jewish War Veterans
of the United States

Institution Program

SYNAGOGUE AHAVATH ACHIM
1741 East 3rd Street
Brooklyn, New York
•
Saturday, October 19, 1946
at 7:30 p. m.

PROGRAM

OPENING .... Lester Sacks
Kings County Exec. Comm.

MASTER OF CEREMONIES .... Saul Nathanson

ADVANCE OF COLORS .... Harry Title
Officer of Day — J. W. V.

NATIONAL ANTHEM .... Murray Wolfson
Kings County Vocalist

INVOCATION .... Rabbi Meyer Karlin

RECEPTION OF GUESTS

INSTITUTION OF POST .... Jack Daniels
Past County Commander

INSTALLATION OF OFFICERS .... Saul Nathanson
Kings County Vice Commander

PRESENTATION OF ALTAR CLOTH .... Irving Polk

ADDRESS .... Benjamin Lewis
Commander

GUEST SPEAKER .... Archie H. Greenberg
Past National Commander

BENEDICTION .... Rabbi Meyer Karlin

CLOSING .... Commander Lewis

ORGANIST .... Samuel Mensch, Ph.D.
Musical Director

Several accounts tell of the fate of Charlie and his crew. The best is from Lawrence J. Hickey and co-authors in, "Ken's Men Against the Empire[16]," substantiated by "Pacific Wrecks[169]." On June 1 Lieutenant Ernest A. Nauman flew Charlie's plane, making his first flight as pilot. Not only didn't the plane return to base, but nothing was known about the fate of the plane or crew until the

Japanese released Sergeant Paul J. Cascio from captivity in Japan after more than two years as a POW.

Cascio reported that three hours into their mission over Gasmata, 12 Japanese fighter planes attacked, hitting the plane's fuel tank so that the rear of the plane trailed flaming gasoline. Pilot Nauman activated flame repression equipment, which worked briefly, but then the fire leapt out of control. Just as Nauman ordered the crew to abandon the plane, it began to disintegrate. Bombardier Lieutenant Oliver Alvin opened the bomb-bay doors and jettisoned the bombs. Cascio and Sergeant Thomas H. Fox stood over the open bomb-bay doors preparing to jump as the plane exploded. Cascio was wearing his parachute. He hesitated to pull the ripcord because he'd heard stories of the Japanese shooting at helpless airmen as they descended from crippled planes. But Cascio engaged his parachute and landed on top of a tree. A Japanese fighter plane descended and shot at him, but Cascio unlatched his straps and fell to the ground, spraining his ankle.

Sergeant Cascio hid for a day and then began to walk. He soon found the bodies of Lieutenants Alvin and Lewis, the bombardier and navigator together in death as they had been in the sky. Neither had been wearing a parachute.

After four days in the jungle, Cascio walked into a native village. The people fed him and then took him to another village, where Cascio was reunited with his crewmates Lieutenant Nauman, Sergeant Fox, and Private Charles H. Green. Fox had burns on his arms, legs, and forehead and Green's right knee was badly injured. Nauman had also seen the bodies of Alvin and

Lewis, as well as those of Sergeants Virgin E. DeVoss, Albert Smith, and Bruno B. Bukalski. No one knew the whereabouts of co-pilot Winslow Gardner.

An English-speaking islander offered to escort the four survivors to the coast, with the hope of getting medical attention for Fox and Green. But the natives betrayed the downed American airmen, instead delivering them to the Japanese. A boat then took all four to a Japanese compound where Fox and Green were to receive "medical aid." Instead, the Japanese murdered Fox and Green and buried them in a bomb crater. The bodies were positively identified after the war.

Nauman and Cascio were blindfolded for several days, while the Japanese interrogated Nauman. The two men were then placed with other Allied POWs, when Cascio contracted malaria. For ten days he survived on water and weevil-infested rice, until a ship took him to the island of Truk on July 17. He had become too weak to answer questions from his Japanese interrogators. Finally Cascio was treated at a hospital and recovered somewhat. On July 27, he was put on another ship, bound for Japan. He ended up at Ofuna prison camp. Cascio didn't fully recover from malaria until an Australian POW treated him. When Cascio was finally released, he made a point of contacting all of the families from his crew of the B-17, including Sadie.

Meanwhile, Lieutenant Nauman was held at a POW camp on Rabaul until November 25, 1943, when the Japanese murdered him and about 40 other prisoners, according to reports from civilians at the camp. The guards told Reverend Joseph Lamarre, one of the civilians present, that the men were being taken to Japan, but later a group of Indian POWs reported that the men had been beheaded. Other reports confirmed that the Japanese beheaded captured Allied prisoners at the base of a volcano near Rabaul.

In 1946, an Australian Air Force search team led by Keith Rundle[169] found the wreckage of Charlie's plane. Then in 1987, a US Army recovery team led by Captain Benny Woodward also located Charlie's plane with plans to return later to do proper forensics analysis. That analysis was complete in 1990. First Lieutenant Charles H. Lewis' remains were found and sent to my family in 1990, and Charlie received proper burial in Mt. Ararat Cemetery, in East Farmingdale, Long Island, NY. The US searchers also (finally) found the remains of Lieutenant Winslow Gardner, and his remains were finally reunited with his family in 1991.

My brother Charles H. Lewis was a reporter for the *Ottawa Citizen* in 1991. He had come across a story about the World War II investigative organization, "Pacific Wrecks," finding the wreckage of Texas #6, my uncle's plane, and also the remains of the one and only crew member not accounted for from Charlie's crash, co-pilot Winslow Gardner. "Remembering is Too Easy," my brother's story in the *Ottawa Citizen*, appeared on November 10, 1991:

> *I'm glad my grandmother wasn't alive when the remains of Lt. Winslow Gardner were found. Gardner's body was discovered earlier this year in the wreckage of a B-17 bomber, found 48 years after it went down in the jungles of New Britain. He was the only member of the 10-man crew who had never been fully accounted for.*
>
> *What they found of Gardner was really no more than*

some pieces of bone and part of a boot. But by some miracle of forensic science a positive identification was made. If my grandmother had been alive she'd have been wondering if they'd found another body among the wreckage, the body of her boy. All she ever really knew is that her son, and my uncle, Lt. Charles Lewis, went missing in action somewhere in the South Pacific in 1943.

I knew something about that plane. I'd been hearing about it all my life. My grandmother always talked to me about the war and the son she lost; probably because I was named after him but also because I was interested in listening to her talk about "my Charlie." The bitterness that ran through that woman was never far from the surface. She hated the Japanese and until the day she died could never understand why we were now their friends.

"Not after what they did to our boys," she would say.

It didn't help that I was born on December 7, 1950 – exactly nine years after the Japanese attacked the American naval base at Pearl Harbor – the anniversary of the day that changed her life forever. If December 7 happened to fall on a school day, our teachers would always start the lesson by asking the obvious question: "Does anyone know what day this is?"

I knew the answer.

What little I know about those next four years I learned from my grandmother and the little bit of investigation I did on my own. No one else spoke very much about the war. Certainly not my father. My father is not one to tell war stories. During all those years I can remember him speaking about the war on maybe a half dozen occasions. And even then it was in bits and spurts, not really a conversation. And except for one that I can remember, he never spoke about his brother. That time we were sitting together in a restaurant. I'd been away from home for two years and I had just turned 23.

"You're the same age my brother was when he went down." And that was that.

My father and his brother were close. I learned that from my grandmother. He still keeps a picture of his brother on his desk and on his night table. Shortly after Pearl Harbor my uncle enlisted in what was then the US Army Air Corps. It was an odd choice considering that as a child he was terrified of escalators. My uncle's squadron was based in a jungle airstrip in New Guinea. I've seen only a few pictures of him from that time. He looked proud and full of purpose. He also looked like he was having a hell of a good time playing the part of the valiant young officer.

On June 1, 1943, on a reconnaissance mission over the Japanese stronghold of Rabaul on New Britain, his plane was attacked by more than a dozen Japanese fighter planes. The lone survivor of the mission was taken prisoner by the Japanese and after the war he filed a report about what happened that day.

"They hit our gas tank, which caused our plane to catch on fire. The fire could not be controlled. Lt. Nauman, our pilot, ordered us to abandon the plane, but before we could do so the plane blew up. I was thrown out by the explosion. So were Lt. Lewis and Lt. Alvin. They did not have their parachutes on..." That last part my grandmother never knew.

A short time after the plane was shot down, she received her first telegram of the war. It simply said that her son was missing in action. The next telegram they received came around Christmas, 1944. By this time my father had survived fighting in France, Belgium, and

Holland. But just after breaking into Germany he too went missing.

There's a picture of my grandmother taken in 1942. She's smiling on the front steps of her 65th Street home. The most remarkable thing is that her hair is dark. It's remarkable because by the end of 1944 her hair had turned completely grey. She received two more telegrams before the war's end. The first told her that my father was in a prisoner of war camp. The fact that he had been wounded in battle and then wounded again during an attempted breakout was kept from her. I think that by 1945 she was better off without that news.

The last telegram came just after the end of the war. It was to tell her that her eldest son had been killed in battle. There were no details except to say his death had been confirmed by the surviving crew member. The telegram offered the deepest of regrets. And that was that. Just over two years ago, shortly after my grandmother passed away, I got a chance to look over some of the correspondence she had saved. It was mostly from my father and uncle from overseas. Their letters were purposely vague and full of forced cheer. The letters, along with the telegrams, were in chronological order. The last letter of the bunch was written in 1946. That letter came from Paul Cascio, the only survivor of my uncle's plane. He was writing from Baltimore to say that he knew her son and he was sorry for her pain and if there was ever anything he could do, just to let him know.

Until I discovered Cascio in the Baltimore phone book about two years ago no one had bothered to get in touch with him. We ended up spending the day together. He told me what happened that day over Rabaul and showed me the report – the one about my uncle blown out of the sky – that he filled out when he was liberated from his prison camp. Cascio really didn't know anyone on the plane very well. It was his first, and as it turned out, his last mission.

He knew that my uncle was killed instantly because he found his body just after the crash. The only crew member whom Cascio never saw was Lt. Winslow Gardner.

Just after my visit with Cascio the strangest thing happened. A bush logger in New Britain discovered the wreckage of my uncle's plane. The story made news for a couple of days. Even CNN picked it up. Cascio sent me some clippings from the Gardner story. As the only surviving member of the crew, he was interviewed for several of the news stories. When I heard about this discovery I decided to contact Gardner's relatives in Utah. I'm not really sure why I did this but I thought it would be worthwhile letting them know what I had learned.

I managed to reach Gardner's sister by telephone in Salt Lake City and we spoke for about half an hour. At the end of our conversation I mentioned something about how hard it was to imagine all those young men having gone through these terrible things. And then she told me this story: The girl her brother was to marry was now, of course, an old woman who had married, had children who in turn had children. But when she heard about the body being found it was as if the 48 years had vanished into a single moment. The disbelief, the anger, and the terrible loss were all happening again. And the agony of it all almost caused her a nervous breakdown.

Time hadn't really healed anything, just buried it.

"It wasn't so much a case of remembering, as never being able to forget."

Acknowledgments

MY GRANDMA SADIE saved everything and somehow all of her documents ended up with me. It was meant to be. There are two great writers in my family. My brother Charlie's accounts of the fate of the crew of Texas #6 opened and closed this book in a way I never could. I also hit the jackpot because I am married to Ricki Lewis, a world-famous science writer. Very few people can edit and even a smaller number enjoy doing it. Ricki took my jumble of facts and made them into something readable (I hope). I also thank my readers–Ralph and Linda Spaulding and Roger and Annette Keen who made lots of helpful suggestions. Finally dad and uncle Charlie, this is my way to honor your sacrifice to your country and one last way for me to pass your story onto future generations.

About the Author

LARRY LEWIS has a PhD in chemistry from Indiana University. He grew up in New York City hearing bits of the history of his father's and uncle's service in World War II, especially the stories from his grandmother Sadie. Larry inherited his grandmother's collection of wartime letters and documents. Once he retired after 32 years at GE Global Research, Larry began his quest to fill in the gaps of the story behind his family's past. He lives in Glenville, NY.

References

[1] Denise Kiernan, "The Girls of Atomic City," (Touchstone, NY, 2013).

[2] Ottawa Citizen, Sunday, November 10, 1991.

[3] Brooklyn Eagle, Nov. 4, 1941.

[4] Brooklyn Eagle, Nov.17, 1941.

[5] NY Times, Nov. 3, 1941.

[6] Brooklyn Eagle, Dec. 5, 1941.

[7] Brooklyn Eagle, Nov. 7, 1941.

[8] Brooklyn Eagle, Nov. 6, 1941.

[9] NY Times, Nov. 14, 1941.

[10] NY Times, Nov. 23, 1941.

[11] NY Times, Nov. 24, 1941.

[12] Bruce Gamble, "Fortress Rabaul," (Zenith Press, Minneapolis, 2010).

[13] https://en.wikipedia.org/wiki/Aviation_Cadet_Training_Program_(USAAF).

[14] https://en.wikipedia.org/wiki/United_States_Army_Air_Forces

[15] W.F. Craven, J.L. Cate, "The Army Air Forces in World War II, Men

& Planes, Vol. 6," U. Chicago Press, 1955.

[16] Lawrence J. Hickey, Steve Birdsall, Madison D. Jonas, Edward M. Rogers, Osamu Tagaya, "Ken's Men Against the Empire," (International Historical Research Associates, Boulder, CO, 2016).

[17] http://www.kensmen.com/jan43.html.

[18] awesomestories.com/asset/view/irving-strobing.

[19] Burton Graham, "None Shall Survive," (F.H. Johnson Pub. Co., Sydney, 1944).

[20] http://www.taphilo.com/history/WWII/Loss-Figures-Aircraft-USA-Training.shtml.

[21] James P. Duffy, "War at the End of the World," (New American Library, NY, 2016).

[22] https://en.wikipedia.org/wiki/SS_Montevideo_Maru.

[23] Michael Claringbould, "Forty of the Fifth," (Aerothentic Publications, Australia, 1999).

[24] James t. Murphy, A.B. Feuer, "Skip Bombing," (Praeger, Westport, CT, 1993).

[25] https://en.wikipedia.org/wiki/Boeing_B-17_Flying_Fortress.

[26] https://airforce.togetherweserved.com/usaf/servlet/tws.webapp. WebApp?cmd=ShadowBoxProfile&type=Person&ID=183092.

[27] Brooklyn Eagle, Jan. 28, 1944.

[28] https://commons.wikimedia.org/wiki/File%3A1943_World_War _II_Japanese_Aeronautical_Map_of_New_Guinea_-_Geographicus_-_NewGuinea14-wwii-1943.jpg.

[29] Charles Lewis' Flight Records, Golden Arrow Research geoff.gentilini@goldenarrowresearch.com.

[30] NY Times, January 1, 1943.

[31] Brooklyn Eagle, January 2, 1943.

[32] Brooklyn Eagle, January 3, 1943.

[33] https://en.wikipedia.org/wiki/Louis_Zamperini.

[34] Laura Hillenbrand, "Unbroken," (Random House, NY, 2010).

[35] Brooklyn Public Library http://bklyn.newspapers.com/image/52648538, Copyright 2016 Newspapers.com.

[36] Brooklyn Eagle, January 5, 1943.

[37] Brooklyn Eagle, January 6, 1943.

[38] Brooklyn Eagle, January 7, 1943.

[39] https://history.state.gov/milestones/1937-1945/casablanca

[40] Brooklyn Eagle, January 8, 1943.

[41] Brooklyn Eagle, January 9, 1943.

[42] Brooklyn Eagle, January 10, 1943.

[43] Brooklyn Eagle, January 11, 1943.

[44] Brooklyn Eagle, January 12, 1943.

[45] Brooklyn Eagle, January 13, 1943.

[46] Brooklyn Eagle, January 14, 1943.

[47] https://en.wikipedia.org/wiki/Saving_Private_Ryan.

[48] Brooklyn Eagle, January 15, 1943.

[49] New York Times, January 16, 1943.

[50] Brooklyn Eagle, January 17, 1943

[51] Brooklyn Eagle, January 18, 1943.

[52] Brooklyn Eagle, January 19, 1943.

[53] NY Times, January 20, 1943.

[54] Brooklyn Eagle, January 21, 1943.

[55] Brooklyn Eagle, January 22, 1943.

[56] NY Times, January 23, 1943.

[57] Brooklyn Eagle, January 24, 1943.

[58] Brooklyn Eagle, January 25, 1943.

[59] Brooklyn Eagle, January 26, 1943.

[60] http://www.kensmen.com/64a25.html.

[61] NY Times, January 29, 1943.

[62] http://www.kensmen.com/feb43.html.

[63] https://commons.wikimedia.org/wiki/File%3APapua_N%C3%BD _Guinea_FO_map.png.

[64] http://www.kensmen.com/

[65] http://b17blackjack.com/crew/mccullar/holsey-mccullar-hastings.html.

[66] Quentin Reynolds, "70,000 to 1," (Pyramid, 1946).

[67] https://en.wikipedia.org/wiki/Forrest_Gump.

[68] https://en.wikipedia.org/wiki/Geneva_Conventions.

[69] Brooklyn Eagle, April 19, 1943.

[70] http://www.kensmen.com/mar43.html.

[71] https://en.wikipedia.org/wiki/Howard_Knox_Ramey.

[72] http://www.faqs.org/espionage/Vo-Z/World-War-II-United-States-Breaking-of-Japanese-Naval-Codes.html.

[73] https://en.wikipedia.org/wiki/Isoroku_Yamamoto.

[74] http://www.kensmen.com/apr43.html.

[75] Andrew Carroll, "Grace Under Fire: Letters of Faith in Times of War," (Crown Publishing, 2007).

[76] https://en.wikipedia.org/wiki/Mascot,_New_South_Wales.

[77] https://en.wikipedia.org/wiki/Battle_of_Brisbane.

[78] Brooklyn Eagle, April 23, 1943.

[79] Brooklyn Eagle, May 3, 1943.

[80] Brooklyn Eagle, April 22, 1943.

[81] https://en.wikipedia.org/wiki/Doolittle_Raid

[82] Brooklyn Eagle, April 27, 1943.

[83] https://en.wikipedia.org/wiki/Warsaw_Ghetto_Uprising.

[84] Bruce Gamble, "Target Rabaul," (Zenith Press, Minneapolis, 2013).

[85] http://www.pacificwrecks.com/people/veterans/kudo/ index.html

[86] NY Times, May 31, 1943.

[87] https://en.wikipedia.org/wiki/Army_Specialized_Training_Program

[88] Gerald Astor, "Terrible Terry Allen," (Ballantine Books, 2003).

[89] Charles H. Norris, "Life in the Army-Letters to Jean," (Xlibris, 2001).

[90] Leo A. Hoegh & Howard J. Doyle, "Timberwolf Tracks," (Washington Infantry Journal Press, Washington, DC, 1946).

[91] John H. Light, "An Infantryman Rembers World War II," Beidel Printing House, Inc., Shippenburgh, PA, 1997.

[92] http://www.hardscrabblefarm.com/ww2/eib_info.htm.

[93] http://www.skylighters.org/encyclopedia/fortyandeight.html

[94] http://www.thegriffon108.com/Articles/Article-Detail/articleid/704/a-brief-history-of-the-104th-training-division-timberwolves-704.

[95] Robert G. Span interview on Nov. 28, 2003, Setauket, NY, DMNA.ny.gov/historic/veterans/transcriptions.

[96] https://en.wikipedia.org/wiki/1st_Armoured_Division_(Poland).

[97] https://en.wikipedia.org/wiki/Rashomon.

[98] Rick Catling in "The Islander," Jan. 27, 2010. Interview with Elroy DeMaria.

[99] https://en.wikipedia.org/wiki/Battle_of_the_Bulge.

[100] http://www.oflag64.us/long-cold-march.html.

[101] http://www.oflag64.us/ewExternalFiles/as_i_remember_it-oflag_and_beyond.pdf.

[102] http://oflag64.us/ewExternalFiles/cochran_alexander-interview.pdf "Military History," Vol. 1, $4, Feb. 1985, pp42-49.

[103] http://www.oflag64.us/ewExternalFiles/corbin_robert-story.pdf.

[104] http://www.oflag64.us/ewExternalFiles/culler_john-letter-account.pdf.

[105] http://www.oflag64.us/ewExternalFiles/drake_jay-guest_of_the_third_reich.pdf.

[106] http://www.oflag64.us/ewExternalFiles/meltesen_clarence_r-routes_1.pdf.

[107] http://www.oflag64.us/ewExternalFiles/lockett_james_w-war_department_document.pdf.

[108] http://www.oflag64.us/ewExternalFiles/goode_paul_r-archive_report.pdf.

[109] http://www.oflag64.us/ewExternalFiles/watts_james_h-diary.pdf.

[110] http://www.oflag64.us/ewExternalFiles/horseshit_and_cobblestones.pdf

[111] http://www.oflag64.us/ewExternalFiles/winter_scene-parts_1_and_2.pdf.

[112] http://ia600204.us.archive.org/31/items/WwiiPowJournalOfThorntonV.Sigler/tvs-6.23.44-6.26.45.pdf

[113] https://en.wikipedia.org/wiki/Red_Cross_parcel

[114] http://www.talkingproud.us/Retired/Retired/Oflag64.html.

[115] Clarence R. Meltensen, "Roads to Liberation from Oflag 64," (Oflag 64 Press, Sanfransisco, 2004).

[116] https://en.wikipedia.org/wiki/Bataan_Death_March.

[117] http://www.talkingproud.us/Retired/Retired/Oflag64_files/the-soviets-attack002c-the-pows-are-moved.pdf.

[118] New York Times, January 21, 1945.

[119] Brooklyn Eagle, January 22, 1945.

[120] Brooklyn Eagle, January 23, 1945.

[121] Brooklyn Eagle, January 24, 1945.

[122] Brooklyn Eagle, January 25, 1945.

[123] New York Times, January 26, 1945.

[124] Brooklyn Eagle, January 27, 1945.

[125] Brooklyn Eagle, January 28, 1945.

[126]New York Times, January 29, 1945.

[127]Brooklyn Eagle, January 30, 1945.

[128] New York Times, January 31, 1945.

[129]Brooklyn Eagle, February 1, 1945.

[130]Brooklyn Eagle February 2, 1945.

[131] New York Times, February 3, 1945.

[132]https://en.wikipedia.org/wiki/Auschwitz_concentration_camp.

[133] Brooklyn Eagle, February 4, 1945.

[134] Brooklyn Eagle, February 5, 1945.

[135]New York Times, February 6, 1945.

[136] Brooklyn Eagle, February 6, 1945.

[137]Brooklyn Eagle, February 7, 1945.

[138]Brooklyn Eagle, February 8, 1945.

[139] Brooklyn Eagle, February 9, 1945.

[140]New York Times, February 10, 1945.

[141] New York Times, February 11, 1945.

[142]New York Times, February 12, 1945.

[143] https://en.wikipedia.org/wiki/Tuskegee_Airmen.

[144]Brooklyn Eagle, February 13, 1945.

[145] Brooklyn Eagle February 14, 1945.

[146]Brooklyn Eagle, February 15, 1945.

[147] Brooklyn Eagle, February 16, 1945.

[148] Brooklyn Eagle, February 17, 1945.

[149]Brooklyn Eagle, February 18, 1945.

[150] Brooklyn Eagle, February 19, 1945.

[151] Brooklyn Eagle, February 20, 1945.

[152] New York Times, February 21, 1945.

[153]New York Times, February 22, 1945.

[154] Brooklyn Eagle, February 23, 1945.

[155] Brooklyn Eagle, February 24, 1945.

[156] Brooklyn Eagle, February 25, 1945.

[157] Brooklyn Eagle, February 26, 1945.

[158] https://en.wikipedia.org/wiki/Hogan's_Heroes.

[159] https://en.wikipedia.org/wiki/Stalag_XIII-C.

[160] Cathryn J. Prince, The Times of Israel, November 30, 2016.

[161] https://en.wikipedia.org/wiki/George_S._Patton.

[162] https://en.wikipedia.org/wiki/Patton_(film).

[163] Charles S. Whiting, "48 Hours to Hammelberg," (iBooks, New York, 1970).

[164] Richard Baron, Major Abe Baum, Richard Goldhurst, "Raid!," (G.P. Putnam's and Son, New York, 1981).

[165] http://wwii-pow-camps.mooseroots.com/l/178/Oflag-13B.

[166] https://en.wikipedia.org/wiki/Stalag_VII-A.

[167] New York Times, March 28, 1945.

[168] http://www.skylighters.org/special/cigcamps/cmplstrk.html

[169] http://www.pacificwrecks.com/aircraft/b-17/41-9244.html

Marilyn Lyon

JOLLY
HOLLY

CPSIA information can be obtained
at www.ICGtesting.com
Printed in the USA
FSHW02n2307091018
52861FS